Book of Answers

Almine

WISDOM FOR THE NEW AGE

Published by Spiritual Journeys, LLC

First Edition June 2016

Copyright 2016

PO Box 300
Newport, Oregon 97365

US toll-free number: 1-877-552-5646

www.spiritualjourneys.com

Cover art by Charles Frizzell

Almine portrait by Benno Klandt

Manufactured in the United States of America

ISBN 978-1-936926-54-1 Hardcover

Table of Contents

Endorsements

*"What a priceless experience to be able to catch a glimpse
into one of the most remarkable lives of our time..."*

H.E. Ambassador Armen Sarkissian,
Former Prime Minister of the Republic of Armenia,
Astrophysicist, Cambridge University, U.K.

*"Almine's gifts as a mystic are a revelation to all who know her.
She is an international phenomenon and certainly deserves to be."*

H.E. Sir Colville Young, G.C.M.G., M.B.E., Ph.D
Governor-General of Belize
Central America

DOWNLOADS AND RESOURCES

For the downloads and additional resources that accompany this book visit:

WWW.IAMPRESENCE.COM/
BOOK-OF-ANSWERS

Introduction

For eons man has been plagued by the mysteries of the universe around him, and the secrets that obscure the reason for his existence. This book delivers many answers that give meaning to life and probe the hidden laws of the Universe. Almine, (widely acknowledged as the leading mystic of our time), shares a wealth of information, and intrepidly delves into the plight of humanity. She offers solutions that will enable a harmonious life of graceful change and peace on Earth.

Discourse 1
The Origin of Heaven and Hell

Q. Where do the pervasive concepts of Heaven and Hell come from? Are there such places?

A. Heaven can be called the planetary reality of the High Mind. Hell is the planetary reality of the subconscious, where our unprocessed terrors are stuffed.

Q. So, what makes 'good people' go to Heaven?

A. A 'good' person is merely someone that lives from their highest truth, their high mind. It varies from person to person. For the Muslim, it's living from the laws of Islam. This creates a passage into the planetary high mind (Heaven).

Q. Who inhabits the planetary subconscious or 'hell'? Those whose self-hatred goes unresolved and who therefore, injure others intentionally on a large scale – like those who plan genocides – not just something committed based on temporary blind spots? What about demons?

A. Yes, they are there too and embody chaos so that it doesn't spill into the reality of the middle mind: everyday life. This reality is for those who run away from their 'inner demons'.

Q. Give an example of 'inner demons'.

A. Unresolved issues that cause us to react without discernment – in other words, they 'pull our strings'.

Q. But, everyone has some of that!

A. Yes, but we're talking about it being their primary, or dominant motivating force.

Q. How does one avoid dying into one of these two possible realities, and what about those who live from their logic?

A. The main and largest group of people falls into this category. There is a spirit world (or more accurately, a soul world) much like this everyday life for those who are guided by their feelings and thoughts. How does one bypass these death bound destinations: through bypassing death. All my books have been dedicated to setting man free from death through resurrection, but especially *The Bridge of No Time,* which has mapped metamorphoses out very carefully.

Q. What is resurrected life like?

A. You metamorphose yourself and your reality by allowing the inspiration of Infinite Intent to be your motivating force. During the metamorphoses process, you live and die simultaneously, by reinventing yourself moment by moment. In other words, you fluidly die to the old way of being, like an ever-changing river.

Q. Have you ever been to Hell?

A. Yes. It's part of what is called the third resurrection (or the descent into Hades). But, Hell cannot hold one that sings the Song of Oneness (Inclusiveness), and wholeness in their cells because they embrace all of life as themselves.

Q. Was there anything that surprised you there, and what was the biggest challenge?

A. It surprised me that genocides that were done with black magic purposes (like the Hitler regime), managed to drain the life force of their victims to such an extent that they were able to trap them in the underworld (or 'Hell') also. The biggest challenge is overcoming the fear by recognizing that the reality is a nightmarish dream that we have created by ourselves. We can also refuse it, stating firmly, "This is not my reality. It is but a dream that I choose to no longer experience or create". Then, eliminate those things from the past that are pulling your strings as also being just a dream. The only thing that matters is this moment in which all things are new.

Q. There's so much said about the power of the moment to shape our reality. What is a moment, and how does it form?

A. A moment is a package of potential, or more accurately, it can be called a brief illumination of a portion of existence that is offering its potential for articulation. We live in a field of possibilities. The moment is a brief illumination of a portion of it. A strobe light is used on a dance floor and gives the impression that the dancers are moving from one static pose to another (like a series of snapshots), instead of in smooth, continuous movements. Moments are the same: they appear as separate illuminations because we have no conscious experience of what happens in the gap between the moments.

THE INTERSECTION OF TWO REALITIES ON
AN INDIVIDUAL MACROCOSMIC LEVEL

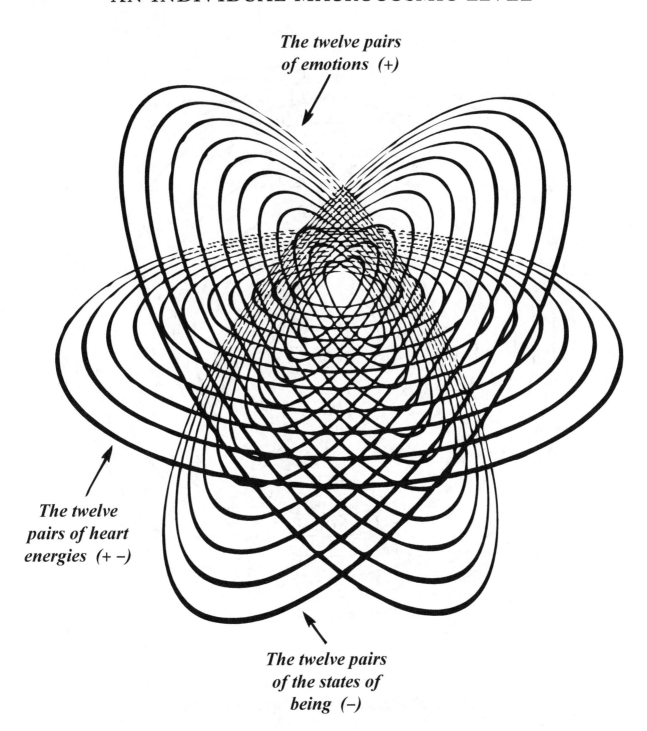

The twelve pairs of emotions (+)

The twelve pairs of heart energies (+ –)

The twelve pairs of the states of being (–)

THE VERTICAL WHEEL IS FORMED BY THE
24 PURE FREQUENCIES OR EMOTIONS

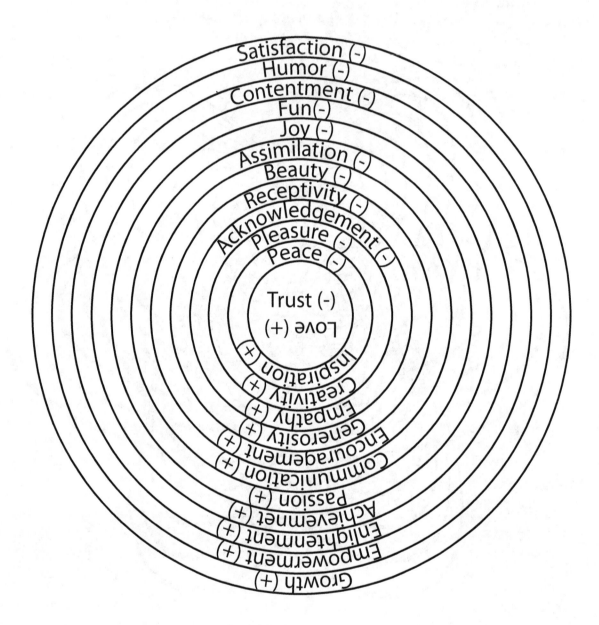

The vertical wheel is formed by 24 emotions.

THE 24 PURE EMOTIONS

1	Trust	The desire to surrender (replaced fear)
	Love	The desire to include
2	Peace	The desire to be at ease, to feel at home (replaced protectiveness)
	Inspiration	The desire to inspire and to be inspired (replaced anger)
3	Pleasure	The desire to be delighted
	Creativity	The desire to create
4	Acknowledgement	The desire to see perfection
	Empathy	The desire to connect
5	Receptivity	The desire to receive
	Generosity	The desire to give
6	Beauty	The desire to be uplifted
	Encouragement	The desire to encourage and to be encouraged
7	Assimilation	The desire to integrate
	Communication	The desire to express
8	Joy	The desire to live
	Passion	The desire to know
9	Fun	The desire to revel
	Achievement	The desire to excel
10	Contentment	The desire to retain
	Enlightenment	The desire to enhance and to be enhanced (replaced pain)
11	Humor	The desire to be amused
	Empowerment	The desire to be of service
12	Satisfaction	The desire to be fulfilled
	Growth	The desire to expand

Q. But, what gives this effect? What causes this selective illumination of portions of existence?

A. The interaction between the body's physical reality and the soul's intangible dream world creates it. The physical reality is like a massive, vertical spinning wheel on a macrocosmic level. Each individuation is experiencing a unique spot on it. This rotates through a static horizontal wheel, or field, that the soul experiences during the dreamtime. When your unique spot on the vertical wheel rotates through your area of awareness on the horizontal wheel, a moment forms. (The vertical wheel illuminates a pocket of potential on the horizontal wheel.)

Q. What makes the vertical wheel move, and is it the same for everyone?

A. The vertical wheel is comprised of 24 Pure Emotions that are based on desire. Desire is a moving force. Strength of desire through these pure frequencies creates a faster spin for some and this creates more possibilities.

Q. Why do healers of the healing modality Belvaspata use the 12 Pairs of Pure Emotions?

A. They move an individual that's stuck in unwholeness into a new range of possibilities, a different reality.

Q. What does the reality of the soul (the static horizontal wheel) consist of?

A. The 24 Principles of Being Home for Oneself. These 24 frequencies are an emphases of the still contentment of the inner world, the inner space. To understand what I am about to explain, the subpersonalities have to be explained: In our daily lives, we live from the Inner Child, Inner Elder (or Sage), Inner Nurturer and Inner Warrior. Each subpersonality emphasizes 6 of the 24 Pure Emotions. When the person becomes a resurrected master, they use the additional 24 Principles of Being Home for Oneself, and new subpersonalities come alive within the psyche. Among these is the Inner Babe. This integrates doingness and beingness, and life and death (which creates a resurrected state). So, now let me explain the new subpersonalities of a resurrected life.

The 24 Pure Principles of Coming Home to Oneself (also known as the Principles of the Inner Babe)

INTRODUCTION

The subpersonalities of the psyche represent the directions, a navigational system with which we decide which qualities of a specific direction we wish to emphasize in the expressions of our lives. The subpersonalities of the Inner Nurturer, Inner Child, Inner Sage and Inner Warrior (the four directions) are used to relate in physical life.

In expanded awareness, three additional directions, or subpersonalities, are used: The High Priest (or high mind, representing the direction of above), the Inner Scout (representing the direction of without), and the Wild Woman (representing the direction of below).

It is only when the master moves into resurrection stages of evolution that the eighth subpersonality (the direction of within) becomes vitally important, the Inner Babe. A resurrected master lives with one foot in Inner Space, or inner awareness. The other foot is in the awareness ,and seven directions, of the master's outer world. The direction of within, represented by the Inner Babe, must therefore be accessible to the master. This is done by accessing and living the 24 qualities of the Inner Babe, the qualities of being home for oneself.

The emphases of the Inner Babe is also very important for the practitioner of High Magic. It is the storehouse of the latent resources a practitioner of High Magic draws from: the resting place of inaction where we gather the strength for potent action. It is the channel for effortless knowing and innate discernment.

The power of the Inner Babe balances the union of the Inner High Priest as it observes the large flow of events, with the inner guidance of inevitable action within the larger arena. This means that the Inner Priest's high-minded vision establishes a parameter within which the Inner Babe can explore its world and its self.

The Inner Babe does not differentiate play from non-play, or duty. It approaches all life with lighthearted wonderment as long as its basic needs are met. To see life through its eyes is to see life anew.

THE 24 PRINCIPLES OF THE INNER BABE

1	The gentle power of pivotal action
2	Latent resources of primal origins
3	The reservoir of gathered strength
4	The Source of authenticity
5	The wellspring of happiness
6	The discovered core of individuation
7	The joyous reunion with the root of individuation
8	The natural expression of unique perspective
9	The innocence of guiltless responses
10	Inevitable action through inspired wonderment
11	The perspective of surrendered curiosity
12	The ultimate marriage of inner and outer realities
13	Deeper exploration of the senses
14	The resting place of inaction
15	The storehouse of inner resources
16	The channel for innate discernment
17	The inalienable, self-contained contentment of being at home
18	Exploration of the self in a designated arena
19	Delightful discoveries of the boundless self
20	Expressing the laughter of the endless adventure
21	The fluid balance of the chosen focus
22	Receptivity to nurturing from the environment
23	Complete confidence in supply
24	The self-sovereignty of pleasing the self

Q. But what is the actual benefit of living the qualities of the Inner Babe?

A. When a subpersonality is unexpressed, it becomes dysfunctional. The Nurturer becomes critical, the Child becomes needy and so forth. The planetary Inner Child is activated when we express ours. When it is dysfunctional, genocides occur.

Q. What has genocide to do with a dysfunctional Inner Babe? You've explained that the underworld forms because the Inner Babe is not expressed. But didn't you previously say it formed because of an unexpressed Inner Child?

A. The Inner Child is about five years old. The Inner Babe is about 18 to 24 months old. 'Hell' or the 'under, underworld' forms because the Inner Babe becomes self-centered, and disregards the effect of his actions on others. I've discovered an underworld beneath (at a lower frequency) than the underworld of the Inner Child.

Q. Wow! That's amazing. Please tell us about the victims of genocides that you found there. What can set them free?

A. In the New Testament, it speaks about "the spirits that are in prison," this refers to them. They are freed, by living and expressing the Inner Babe because they represent that imprisoned part of ourselves.

Q. Where is the under-underworld?

A. In Earth's Inner Space.

The Self Wheels

An individuation within the limitless ocean of existence has 144 facets, like a beautiful gem cut to perfection. When any one of these aspects, or facets, is not expressing, distortions arise in a person in the form of occlusions (illusions).

These Self Wheels* represent the 144 qualities of individuation. They are sacred objects touching the very heart of the creation of an individual; a unique expression of Infinite design.

---

* To download the Self Wheels, visit: www.alminediary.com/self-wheels

1. Wheel of Adoration of the Infinite

2. Wheel of Highly Refined Frequency and Light

3. Wheel of Ultimate Refinement of Life

4. Wheel of Passionate Exploration

5. Wheel of Self-Exploration

6. Wheel of Gratification in Beingness

7. Wheel of Self-Courage

8. Wheel of Self-Sufficiency

9. Wheel of Self-Knowledge

10. Wheel of Self-Gratitude

11. Wheel of Self-Praise

12. Wheel of Self-Celebration

13. Wheel of Self-Beauty

14. Wheel of Self-Grace

15. Wheel of Self-Sustenance

16. Wheel of Integrated Oneness

17. Wheel of Fire Within

18. Wheel of Self-Truth

19. Wheel of Self-Trust

20. Wheel of Self-Generated Resources

21. Wheel of Entrained Frequency

22. Wheel of Innocence

23. Wheel of Purity

24. Wheel of Adoration in Action

25. Wheel of Regeneration

26. Wheel of Self-Respect

27. Wheel of Self-Directed Desires of the Heart

28. Wheel of Joy in Creation

29. Wheel of Self-Mastery in Action

30. Wheel of Self-Seeing Perfection

31. Wheel of Compassionate Understanding

32. Wheel of Self-Confidence

33. Wheel of Self-Acceptance

34. Wheel of Clarity

35. Wheel of Self-Belief

36. Wheel of Self-Determination

37. Wheel of Interconnectedness

38. Wheel of Self-Motivation

39. Wheel of Pristine Coexistence with Nature

40. Wheel of Self-Accomplishment

41. Wheel of Self-Love in Doingness

42. Wheel of Self-Light in Beingness

43. Wheel of Self-Perception

44. Wheel of Unlimited Access to Knowledge

45. Wheel of Experiential Knowledge

46. Wheel of Self-Dignity

47. Wheel of Fluidity in Mastery

48. Wheel of Self-Discovery

49. Wheel of Devoted Service to the Infinite

50. Wheel of Appreciation of Self-Perfection

51. Wheel of Appreciating Self in External Beauty

52. Wheel of Plentiful Supply

53. Wheel of Appreciating Beauty

54. Wheel of Self-Guidance

55. Wheel of Self-Acknowledgement

56. Wheel of Self-Generated Focus in Life

57. Wheel of Peaceful Desires of the Heart

58. Wheel of Balance in Motion

59. Wheel of Alliances with Infinite Intent

60. Wheel of Self-Appreciation

61. Wheel of Self-Responsibility

62. Wheel of Self-Reliance

63. Wheel of Acknowledging Self-Contributions

64. Wheel of Seeing the Value of All Life

65. Wheel of Unified Fields

66. Wheel of Exponential Growth

67. Wheel of Self-Awareness

68. Wheel of Birthing New Paradigms

69. Wheel of Self-Empowerment

70. Wheel of Purification through Gratitude

71. Wheel of Luminous Living

72. Wheel of Self-Recognition of Uniqueness

73. Wheel of Integrated Sub-personalities

74. Wheel of Embracing Life

75. Wheel of Inclusiveness

76. Wheel of Self-Purity

77. Wheel of Enthusiastic Surrender to the Now

78. Wheel of Self-Nurturing

79. Wheel of Self-Stability through Faith

80. Wheel of Self-Assurance through Humility

81. Wheel of Listening with the Heart

82. Wheel of Delighted Self-Expression

83. Wheel of Self-Encouragement

84. Wheel of Moving Horizons

85. Wheel of Cooperative Endeavors

86. Wheel of Communion with Nature

87. Wheel of Exploration of Self through Others

88. Wheel of Acknowledging Self-Divinity

89. Wheel of Interpretative Dance

90. Wheel of Appreciative Awareness of Details

91. Wheel of Efficient Use of Resources

92. Wheel of Humble Assimilation of New Potential

93. Wheel of Countless Achievements

94. Wheel of Expanded Aspirations

95. Wheel of Deepening Experiences

96. Wheel of Fluidly Shifting Consciousness

97. Wheel of Self-Wisdom

98. Wheel of Self-Assessment

99. Wheel of Simplicity of Choices

100. Wheel of Freedom from Nostalgia of the Past

101. Wheel of Collaboration to Do Life-Enhancing Work

102. Wheel of Creating New Memories

103. Wheel of Boundless Growth through Grace

104. Wheel of Individual Relationship with the Infinite

105. Wheel of Abundant Living

106. Wheel of Joyful Journey of Discovery

107. Wheel of Emotional Self-Fulfillment

108. Wheel of New Creations

109. Wheel of All-Encompassing Presence

110. Wheel of Releasing Duty

111. Wheel of Releasing Resistance

112. Wheel of Authenticity

113. Wheel of Self-Manifested Intent

114. Wheel of One Heart-Mind

115. Wheel of Pristine Creations

116. Wheel of Imaginative Expression

117. Wheel of Expanding Inner Sight

118. Wheel of Heaven on Earth

119. Wheel of Acknowledging Earth's Divinity

120. Wheel of Communion with the Infinite

121. Wheel of Complete Release

122. Wheel of Deeper Understanding of the Infinite

123. Wheel of Dissolving Obsolete Patterns

124. Wheel of Unlimited Learning

125. Wheel of Dissolving Dysfunctionality

126. Wheel of Complete Trust in Divine Order

127. Wheel of Flowering

128. Wheel of Honoring Diversity

129. Wheel of Oneness with the Infinite

130. Wheel of Full Emotional Expression

131. Wheel of Eternal Life

132. Wheel of Creating Sacred Space

133. Wheel of Physical Manifestation

134. Wheel of Restoration to Magical Life

135. Wheel of Mastery of Alchemy

136. Wheel of Becoming Divine Architects

137. Wheel of Instant Access to Infinite Knowledge

138. Wheel of Restoration of Magical Kingdoms

139. Wheel of Dissolving Stagnant Boundaries

140. Wheel of Dissolving Programming

141. Wheel of Perfect Harmony

142. Wheel of Limitless Creativity

143. Wheel of Unobstructive Vision

144. Wheel of Everlasting Guidance by the Infinite

THE ORIGINS OF PREJUDICE

Q. You have said before that tribalism originates from the planetary or individual Inner Child's need to belong. That its search for uniformity within the tribe comes from the Inner Child seeking sameness in the mirrors of its relationships in its search for identity. What social manifestations can we see that represent the Inner Babe?

A. The answer to this question will also clarify why the unexpressed and dysfunctional Inner Babe can create genocides: The social stage of the Inner Babe is tribes, based on value. This can become distorted when tribes try to annihilate those seen as being of lesser value in the tribe's eyes, and genocides result. An example is the Jews versus the Aryan race, another would be Aboriginals exterminated by 'civilized' conquerors.

Q. And this has formed the under, underworld?

A. In the individual it forms a sub-subconscious.

Q. How can this be purified in the individual, which I assume will also heal and liberate souls captured there on a planetary basis?

A. Well, other than studying and expressing the qualities of the Inner Babe that I previously mentioned, there is a very large contribution that the individual can make: It hinges on knowing the infinite value of the self and others as expressions of the One Life. The life's philosophy changes from, "I'm acceptable, you're not acceptable," to "I'm acceptable, and you're acceptable".

Q. So finding self-worth cannot come by diminishing others?

A. We are judgmental of others when our value is based on comparisons. The root of judgmentalness is to elevate our own worth. Find the self-worth and judgmentalness melts away.

Q. If the purpose of the subconscious is to store self-doubt and self-hatred, what is the purpose of the high mind?

A. It holds the vision that sustains your reality, and prompts with the voice of conscience when you stray from the game plan of your life. The subpersonality it represents is the Inner High Priest.

Q. What happens when it is not lived, and it's dysfunctional?

A. The qualities of the High Priest when lived, create a fluid, designated arena of expression (a fluid reality) in which specific aspects of existence are explored.

When dysfunctional, it becomes a moralistic, rigid dictator. Religions replace spirituality and judgmentalness returns. It is meant to hold a larger vision and allow the adventure of exploration to unfold, not to dictate how it should unfold.

Discourse 2
Beyond the Human Paradigm

Q. What is so disturbing to observing the old and infirm? It's almost as though they remind us of our mortality.

A. It is a depressing thought that a life well lived should come to such an ignoble and decrepit end. Furthermore, the thought that all they have to look forward to is death strengthens the illusion of its inevitability. The truth is that the seeming reality of such decay and ultimate death is ingrained in us only because there aren't enough role models to show us anything to the contrary, and the way of death and decay is exemplified by the masses.

Q. Why is the road to incorruptibility so obscured?

A. There are a couple of reasons. Firstly, the things of the world and its value systems are of very little importance to someone who lives beyond the grid of humanity, beyond the paradigm of the masses. The master therefore doesn't usually exhibit excellence in areas that the rest of humanity values.

Q. So their greatness isn't observable to humanity, being outside of their paradigm?

A. Yes. Secondly, the ones the world thinks of as 'great' all end up in the grave, so either it gives the impression that it's the only option open because even the 'great' ones ended up there, or that greatness is only found in those who lived in the past.

Q. This road to incorruptibility – is there any other reason why it's so hidden?

A. The hedonistic qualities found in youth demand that the young not concern themselves with old age but instead, live as though there is no tomorrow. But, you're correct: this is a road and not a destination. Immortality isn't about old age or youth, or retaining the freshness and beauty of the young – these are side effects, fringe benefits of a life well lived.

Q. Are you saying that decay and old age are signs that life was not well lived?

A. Actually, yes, but that's only because the world doesn't understand the meaning of the words 'well lived'. They think it means how pious the person was, how charitable to others, how hard working in raising their children, how much they've achieved, and leaving the world a better place.

Q. Well, doesn't it? Doesn't it all add up to how much we've contributed to making the world a better place?

A. No, it doesn't. Creation doesn't require that man improve it and reality cannot be fixed or changed by us for others. It is arrogance to suppose the Infinite waits for us to perfect Creation. The only thing we can shape and mold with our choices, is our own reality.

Q. Then what is the goal of a life well lived?

A. Claiming the self-sovereignty of being the maker of our own reality and breaking free from a belief system that gives its power away to death.

Q. What qualities does the body need to acquire to become free from death?

A. It has to become self-regenerating. Let's look at what we mean by that, because in a way it still sounds as if this implies 'fixing' or improving part of creation (namely our body). It means to expose the eternalness of our being by continually removing the world's limiting beliefs, and releasing resistance to life.

Q. But isn't opposition caused by resistance a law of physics; a necessary part of creating directional movement like the friction beneath ones feet?

A. For the master, resistance as a way of movement is not an option. The master doesn't move in a different direction because he's moving away from opposition. The master senses the subtle tension created when inspiration beckons him to express greater excellence in some aspect of his life, and guides his course.

Q. What is excellence exactly? We know that you have said opposition is a mirror, or confining matrix, formed by our judgments of what is worthy or life enhancing, and what is not.

A. Inspiration is the stirring of the inner sense in response to the Infinite's whispered intent. It beckons us to increase the illumination in certain parts of our life's journey.

Q. How do we break free from the world's limiting belief systems?

A. Our outer senses are being bombarded by the world's paradigms. Firstly, when people judge us by our age or impose other limiting belief systems on us, it adds to the difficulty of living 'outside the box'. Remove yourself from uninspiring situations and relationships. Be aware of others draining your energy. It will produce tension in your body to be with them and unauthentic behavior (also indicated by bodily tension) as you try and live up to their expectations. So, first rule of thumb is interacting sparingly with the world. When you express your inner subpersonalities, you find fulfillment in your own company. It's no longer a need to be with others to keep you from being lonely. The criteria becomes that you're with someone because they inspire you.

Q. What could prevent our bodies from becoming self-regenerating?

A. The war we wage against our own bodies interrupts its self-love message, that it is worthy and lovable as it is, and worth perpetuating.

Q. Explain how we wage a war against our own bodies please.

A. We like this part, but not that part; we hate this wrinkle, or that pocket of fat. We use (often very toxic) beauty products to change our appearance. Some are obsessed with building the body into a shape that it is not naturally. Or we eat too much, too little, or foods that are hostile to the body. We over-medicate, fearing germs and not trusting our own body's resilience and support, which it would gladly give if we love, accept and support it.

Q. There is a biblical scripture that says, "The wages of sin are death." Why is there such a persistent train of thought in many cultures that death and sin are linked?

A. They are indeed, but the original meaning of the word 'sin' has been distorted. It means to oppose the will of the Infinite, which as we've seen means to ignore the guidance of what elevates our vision and inspires excellence.

Q. So it doesn't have the punitive meaning that we have come to associate with it? Yet it leads to death?

A. We shape the decrepit body of old age, that is so devoid of life force that the soul eventually leaves, and the body no longer is able to sustain itself. The life force leaves in increments every time we oppose life, or try and control external circumstances. All we can control is our response to life. The body withers when we harbor negative thoughts and feelings, and flourishes from love, praise and gratitude. This affects the condition of the body, the way that a river carves the rocks over time.

Q. We can't just decide to claim our incorruptibility at the end of our lives; it's a life-long process?

A. It's always possible to achieve incorruptibility. It is done one pure thought after another or through a miraculous epiphany of perception. It's just that the latter way is very difficult to do if someone's thoughts are cluttered with belief systems.

Q. What is it like to have an uncluttered mind?

A. It is to live with the wonderment of a child at life's miraculous unfoldment. But living in this world, programmed thinking creeps in like weeds into a very well tended garden and it is necessary to be constantly watchful.

Q. How?

A. By living the observer and the observed, we become aware of the origin of our actions. Are they conditioned by belief systems, or do they arise from the wellspring of inspiration? A dysfunctional Inner Nurturer will indulge weak, self-disempowering thoughts by justifying or excusing them. Be diligent about this occurring.

The Total Commitment

Q. Some people have suffered so much in life that death seems like a welcome release?

A. If the magnificent goal of incorruptibility is to be achieved, the commitment to life has to be total. There are several fallacies about the illusion you mentioned: Firstly, death is a little like a hotel with mediocre rooms and service, with a very welcoming and grand foyer. Those who've had a 'near death experience', a peek into the foyer of the hotel of death, describe it as a place of release from suffering and a place of ultimate peace. This is an illusion. The life in the soul world is similar to here, except that the suffering is more emotional. Life is very controlled there, with less freedom of individual choice.

Q. Then what is the solution?

A. To overcome death, the answer is to enter incorruptibility…

Q. Excuse me, but what is the difference between incorruptibility and immortality?

A. Immortality delays death (which is a purification rite) by purifying each day. It cannot delay it indefinitely. Incorruptibility uses the process of resurrection to integrate the two opposites of life and death so that birth, rebirth and death can't repeat in cycles over and over again. (See the book *The Bridge of No Time*, by the Seer Almine, available at https://www.spiritualjourneys.com.) Incorruptibility not only requires daily purification of the world's belief systems, but also daily new insights of life's original oneness.

Q. In other words we shed worldly programs but replace them with new insights of the unpolluted aspect of existence?

A. Yes. This is where we have to decide to release any attractive illusions that the duality of life and death can ever bring lasting peace. Only a total commitment to eternal life, born of daily dying to our old self and old worldviews can carry us further.

Q. What is the main self-defeating attitude that keeps us bound to mortality?

A. Feeling self-pity because of victimhood.

Q. How do we overcome it, when there is always the risk of something bad happening looming as a possibility?

A. The possibility of risk is vastly overemphasized if risk means unwarranted and unnecessary suffering. The chances of that are nil.

Q. Are you saying that suffering is always deserved?

A. You are still entrenched in the worldview that suffering is punitive. Exactly the optimum amount of discomfort is produced to steer our lives in the desired direction in which life's opposition doesn't produce more hardship than we can bear; where it breaks us down instead of strengthening us.

Q. A hardship somewhere prevents a hardship somewhere else?

A. Yes, it prevents inner or outer damage by presenting an opportunity to expand awareness.

Why Death is Not the Answer

AN INTERVIEW WITH THE SEER ALMINE
BY RONNI NAGGAR

Q. There seems to be a tremendous rise in suicide statistics, as well as self-injury, which has become a sort of fashion among the young. Can you give us some answers during this interview to firstly understand death, and secondly, to comprehend why death is not the answer?

A. The place to start might be to understand what death is, and where someone goes when they die. The dream world is entered when the dream body (which is the same as the soul) leaves the physical body to have experiences in a parallel reality (the soul world). During dreaming it is attached by a cord to the physical body. During death, that cord breaks and awareness is drawn away from the physical body, which then decays.

Q. Not many teachers have spoken about the dream world and the soul world, or place of death, as the same…

A. Yes, it eluded me for years as well, until I did an intense study for a week with five students in my home, following them into their dream worlds.

Q. Is it this idyllic place that we believe it to be, and how does death of natural causes occur?

A. Well, let's look at the second question first. The awareness particles, or sub-atomic particles of which formed life consists, are stuck to one another like spiraling ropes. They pummel the fields around the body and the body itself. The Toltecs call this grinding action against the individual, "The Tumbler" – their name for death. The more we resist life, the more we pit ourselves against The Tumbler and hasten death. The fields around the body resemble a luminous egg. This luminous cocoon eventually cracks from the grinding force, and death occurs.

Q. And what about the first part of my question?

A. Life in the mirrored world of duality bounces between three mirrors: life, death and ascension. Mirrors lie, promising to deliver what they can't…

Q. What does death promise to give but then does not?

A. Peace, an end to suffering. The karma of deeds has to be resolved in the physical. The karma of emotions has to be resolved in the soul realms. We can decrease this, by heeding and resolving the messages of our dreams. So, while our physical discomfort may decrease after death, our emotional discomfort increases.

Q. Just as an aside, what karma do we have to solve in the ascension realms?

A. Regrets and chances we believe we missed.

Q. If the dream world and the soul world are the same, doesn't that mean we can visit those who have passed on during our sleep?

A. That is exactly what it means.

Q. What is the fate of those who commit suicide?

A. In one way or another, all death is suicide, in that it is a voluntary choice. The only difference is that intense emotions of despair and hopelessness will have to be resolved and overcome in the soul world by someone committing suicide, when in fact they are trying to escape them.

Q. We seem to have covered what death is, and where we go when we die, and why it doesn't bring the relief we seek…Why the increase in self-inflicted death?

A. There are multiple reasons converging presently. One is the irresponsible messages of the media and their unquenchable desire to report only bad news, rather than the victories of man. Media entertainment is primarily centered around death, violence or conflict. Carefully choose what you and your children watch.

Q. What other reasons are there?

A. Suicidal tendencies come as a result of the blockage of the thyroid meridian, also known as the triple warmer meridian. Some contributing factors are toxicity from consuming impure foods, using toxic cosmetics that are absorbed through the skin, and stress. The most effective product we have found is a pure essential oil from Arabia, which comes from the agar tree, called Oud. (Please note: the quality of this oil varies widely. Almine recommends the oil on FragranceAlchemy.com called The Blend of the Gods.)

Q. I am not clear why a fragrant oil would help alleviate suicidal tendencies, and also, where should it be applied?

A. The olfactory sense is the one sense that never fell (lowered in frequency). The calling of an individual from one mirror, namely life, to another, which is death, is a game of mirrors and duality. Smell can remind us of a timeless existence before life fell into duality, especially if the potency of an essential oil is alchemically enhanced. Even wearing it in the presence of another can assist them, but it can be applied to the outside of the wrist where the two bones of the forearm meet.

Q. What other reason is there for the increase in suicidal tendencies?

A. Drug usage, anti-depressants and other mood altering substances that create a fake feel-good mood, tell the brain that it doesn't have to produce its own. Seratonin production slows down and depression takes over. Some very good homeopathic products exist to help kick-start this back into production. (Note: Almine recommends Psy-stabil, a spagyric homeopathic. This product can be ordered at 1-877-552-5646 in the US).

Q. In closing, let me ask you a very pointed question. Besides from understanding that one of the good reasons to live is that there is not a good reason to die, what makes living a good choice?

A. Firstly, the soul realms are a reality that is just as controlled and regimented in regards to the freedom of an individual as the physical realms are – it isn't really an escape. Secondly, the journey of the ages from life to death, and occasionally through ascension, is a depressing prospect by itself. It creates a deep-seated hopelessness that, like a rat on a treadmill, we cannot escape its seemingly endless control.

But the tremendously hopeful message is that we can, and the place from which to achieve this is from physicality – the conditions under which we are most likely to have success. There is a clear path that has emerged for the first time since the end of 2012, guiding us to return to the indivisible, timeless existence of our true being. It is from this sublime state that we can interact with the real in our fellow man, without entering into their illusions and mirrored worlds.

Q. Thank you so much for this clarity.

Discourse 3
Mystical Secrets of the Human Form

Q. Why has the global population urbanized to the extent that man has become cut off, a stranger from nature in many ways?

A. He feels that nature is hostile, and not a reliable support system. He bands together in cities and creates a predictable support system, which uses civilization as a protection against nature.

Q. So he becomes destructive to nature because he sees nature as hostile to him?

A. Yes. The reason he views nature as unsupportive is because of viewing his body as such. As we see our body, so we shall see nature. Our bodies are after all, part of nature, and not separate from the many other creatures found in nature.

Q. In what way is the body seen as unsupportive?

A. We believe that the body needs to be controlled rather than trusted. It is believed to be vulnerable to invasion from germs, incapable of producing its own nutrition or of self-regenerating areas of injury or atrophy. We believe that the body cannot fend for itself, so we try and compensate for areas that we believe are vulnerable, which makes it more incapable, until it feels as though we are trying to plug the holes in a sieve.

Q. We believe the body may manifest ill health at any time, while we want optimum function of our bodily systems. This creates a conflict.

A. Yes, it's no wonder that the body becomes an opposite to our desires and that our peace is disturbed by its opposition.

Q. What is the result of seeing the body as an opposite?

A. Opposites arise from judgment and teach us through opposition.

Q. How does the 'language of pain' factor into the picture?

A. The way to deal with opposition is to turn it into an ally rather than an opponent. If we reside in a reality in which we see our body as an opposite, we have to turn it into our ally. The Toltec Mystics call it 'stealing death's allies'. Death uses hardships to wear us down and make us want to leave this life.

The Language of Pain

MESSAGES OF THE ORGANS OF THE BODY

Breath indicates our ability to express ourselves in life. If we don't express ourselves, it is as though someone has placed a boulder on our chest and we cannot fully breathe. Frequently, people place the boulder on themselves.

The breath is expressing our life force, so **asthma** patients have life force problems. Often they were stifled from expressing as children. Babies and toddlers know the big picture of who they are, so they may experience tremendous frustration over being trapped in a physical body, unable to express the glory of their true identity. It is helpful to assist children to find safe avenues to explore their gifts and talents. When the life force becomes suppressed, the exhaling process becomes difficult, as is the case with asthma.

The **fluids** of our body have to do with emotions. **Blood,** in particular, is the equivalent of love. The ability to love is very important. If we deliberately withhold love we find constriction in our arteries. **Hardened arteries** mean hardened emotions and condition of love.

The **heart** has to do with giving love. Drawing love from the limitless supply of the universe it should flow out through our heart. If we close our heart because of fear or from not being fully present in our body, then we begin to give energy from our life force center. This depletes us.

In order to insulate ourselves from this drain of energy, a layer of fat could build up around the solar plexus (stomach area). Light workers frequently have this layer of fat as an attempt to protect their energy source. People who suffered childhood abuse may use fat to insulate themselves from other people.

It is important to live fully in the body. Many people have suffered childhood sexual abuse and learned to leave the body when things got unpleasant. If we don't stay in the body and feel, then the heart center remains closed and we cannot fulfill our highest calling on this planet.

Soft tissues and ligaments reflect attitudes. Is our attitude positive? Do we frequently complain? The **joints** have to do with how flexible we are. The soft tissues control the joints, so they are affected too. For example, in the past, prior to a seminar I would receive the topic but no specific information on the forthcoming lecture. As a result, my knee joints hurt because I wasn't flexible enough to trust that I would receive the information at the appropriate time.

The **skin** reflects how we interface with the world. When the skin is irritated, it is because we perceive the world as abrasive or hostile. If a **boil** develops, that means a specific area of our life is like a sore.

Bones indicate what we inherited from our parents and ancestors, or what we received from genetic memory and early social conditioning.

If an ailment occurs on the **front** of the body, that means we are aware of the issue but we haven't dealt with it yet. If the ailment is on the **back** of the body, we are trying to put it behind us, or we aren't aware of it yet. If it is on the **left side** of the body, it has to do with our feminine aspects, or with female relationships in our life. Problems on the **right side** of the body reflect the masculine part of ourselves, or our masculine relationships.

A **virus** is the result of being invaded—our boundaries have broken down. The first and foremost sacred space for us is our body and we honor ourselves by establishing healthy boundaries and maintaining it.

Viruses, bacteria and fungus invade when our subpersonalities aren't healthy, happy, whole and functioning. Fungus tends to come when we have abandoned ourselves, bacteria invades when deliberate hostile influences are entering our boundaries and viruses are the result of others being allowed to use and abuse us.

ANATOMY — DREAM SYMBOLS
(EXCERPT FROM *Labyrinth of the Moon, 2nd Edition*)

Anatomy	
Achilles heel	an unresolved area of your life, unyielded insights
Ankles	flexibility in moving forward in daily life <ul><li>left – feminine aspects or relationships of life, such as spirituality</li><li>right – masculine aspects or relationships of life</li></ul>
Appendix	something unnecessary
Arms	the way others treat you or you treat others <ul><li>right – males, left – females</li></ul>
Back	<ul><li>upper – responsibility or ability to carry workload</li><li>mid – expression, self-expression</li><li>lower – support or lack of</li></ul>
Back of head	let go of old memories
Belly button	sustenance or life force
Belly	the need for approval and/or nurturing
Blood	love
Bones	parental and hereditary information
Breath	expressing life force
Breasts	nurturing or need of
Buttocks	sexuality
Calves	self-perceived destiny
Chest (lungs)	self-expression when expelling the breath, pent-up grief
Colon	letting go of what no longer serves us
Coccyx bone	imposed beliefs of destiny through past lives

Dark skin	the sub-personalities of the inner sage and inner child
Duodenum/ Transverse colon	mothering or insufficient mothering (solar plexus area)
Ears	desire or ability to hear
Ears on other parts of the body	listen to language of your pain
Elbows	fluidity in how we treat others
Eyebrows	articulating self-expression to others
Eyes	desire or ability to see
Eye/one on the forehead	desire for intuitive knowing
Face	how you present yourself to others
Feet	ability to move forward
Forehead	foresight needed
Gallbladder	ability to process density
Genitals	• self – self-perception of one's maleness or femaleness • other's – one's maleness/femaleness as reflected by another
Hair	social self-image
Hands	relationships
Head	intuition, idealism, thought
Heart	ability to give love
Hips	where the way we desire to move through life and the way we are moving through life meet
Kidneys	fear
Knees	flexibility with relationships and our required roles • left – feminine, right – masculine
Legs	progress through life
Lips	verbal communication, verbal manipulation

Liver	anger
Moles on skin	protective mechanisms of social mannerisms
Mouth	ability to receive sustenance
Nails	need to defend
Neck	ideals versus reality; the place where the way we want life to be and the way it seems to be, meet
Nose	the right to happiness, to flourish; personal power
Ovaries/testicles	procreation or offspring
Pancreas	appreciative perspectives
Pubis/pelvic bone	protecting sexuality
Rectum	ability to manifest self-sustenance and abundance
Shoulders	responsibility
Skeleton	basic parental social conditioning
Skin interaction	with others and outside circumstances
Skull	individuated expression
Spine	self-reliance
Spleen	safeguard your resources
Stomach	acceptance of life's circumstances
Teeth	need for aggression • falling out - no need for aggression • being brushed - getting ready for a battle • cavities – having the belief that aggression is needed
Thighs	sexuality
Throat	unspoken or spoken words
Toe(s)	(see Mayan glyphs for fingers and toes)
Tongue	speech
Wrists	fluidity in relationships

The Language of the Fingers and Toes

BODY PARTS AS DREAM SYMBOLS (EXCERPT FROM *Labyrinth of the Moon, 2nd Edition*)

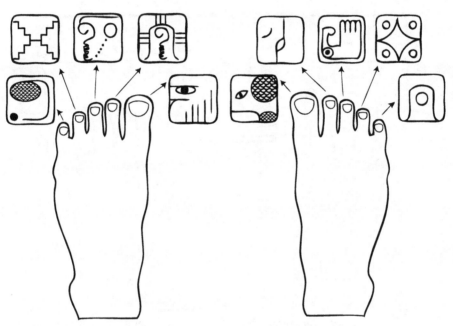

 Storm - *catalyzes, energy, self-generation*

 Moon - *universal water, purification, flow*

 Mirror - *reflects, endlessness*

 Star - *elegance, art, self-expression*

 Earth - *synchronicity, evolves, navigation*

 Hand - *knows, accomplishment, giving and receiving*

 Warrior - *questions, fearlessness, intelligence*

 World Bridger - *equalizer, death, opportunity*

 Earth - *creates, vision, perspective*

 Serpent - *survives, life force, instinct*

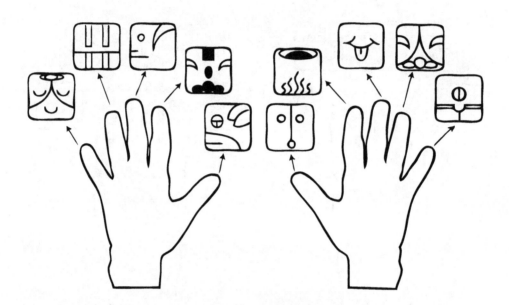

 Wizard - *receptivity, timelessness*

 Seed - *flowering, intention, parable telling*

 Skywalker - *explore, wakefulness, pierce the veil*

 Night - *abundance, sanctuary, retreat*

 Human - *influences, wisdom, free will*

 Wind - *communication, spirit, breath*

 Monkey - *play, childlike innocence, illusion, trickster*

 Dragon - *primal matrix, space*

 Dog - *loyalty, relationship, partners of destiny*

 Sun - *enlightens, elegance, ascension, universal fire*

Q. How does it do that?

A. The way to turn a pain into perception is to learn the language of pain. Disease and pain can only occur when we have forgotten our inclusiveness and oneness with a certain part of existence – the language of pain tells us which part.

Q. Would you tell me more about the connection between the body and the Earth?

A. It's as if all life forms are connected with an underlying language or code. For instance, the shape of a forest plant's leaves can tell you what organ it will either beneficially or detrimentally affect. Wild foxglove has heart-shaped leaves. The leaves can stop a heart and are used in cardiac medicine to control irregular heartbeats and strengthen heart contractions (the medication is Digitalis). Our body also mimics certain places on Earth.

Q. Such as…?

A. Well, let's just look at the skull. It has 13 sections of bone, and 13 main acupressure points. It is a miniature replica of the Earth itself, which has 13 tectonic plates. Native tribes call the Earth Turtle Island because like a turtle that has a shell consisting of twelve segments around the thirteenth, the Earth's tectonic plates are also twelve around the globe, and the thirteenth is found inside the hollow Earth.

Q. You have mapped out the sigils of the Points of Ikelke: the power points of the skull. Alchemical rose oil can be used on these points to overcome birth trauma, and as a rejuvenating tool. What do they represent?

A. An octave on the piano consists of 13 half tones. The 13 sections of the skull, just like the 13 sections of the Earth, each have a different tone. They are like musical notes that you activate when you use the sigils, with each representing a unique passive (feminine) and active (masculine) quality.

Q. What else should we know in working with the Sigils of Ikelke?

A. Like all sacred tools, the sigils themselves hold power, but it is in living the principles that they embody that we become masters of these tools.

Q. Rose oil that has been alchemically prepared (see www.fragrancealchemy.com) can heal birth trauma. What is our relationship with the plants?

A. For every physical infirmity and deficiency there is a plant somewhere that can heal it. The plants carry the notes to the Song of Oneness. Diseased areas of the body arise when parts of the body forget their oneness and wholeness. This is often the result of judgment, our dissatisfaction with our body.

REMOVING BIRTH TRAUMA AND OTHER
GENETIC MEMORIES FROM THE SKULL

To remove birth trauma and other genetic memories from the skull, apply one drop of Rose Oil on each of the 13 points on the face and head. As you apply the oil, either look at the relevant sigil for that point, or run your index finger from left to right over the sigil. You may use the index finger of either hand.

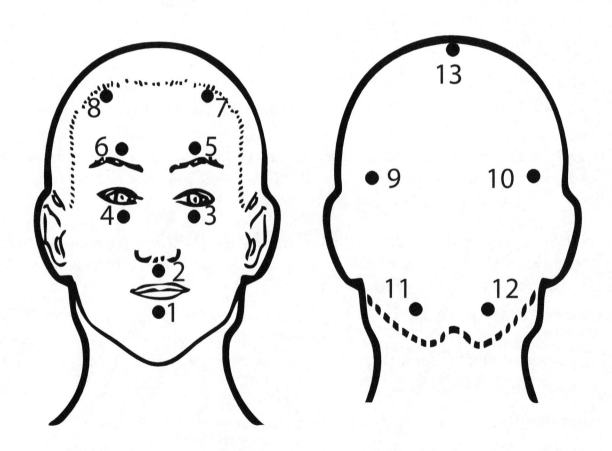

SIGILS FOR THE REMOVAL OF BIRTH TRAUMA
AND GENETIC MEMORIES FROM THE SKULL

Sigil for Point 1

Sigil for Point 6

Sigil for Point 11

Sigil for Point 2

Sigil for Point 7

Sigil for Point 12

Sigil for Point 3

Sigil for Point 8

Sigil for Point 13

Sigil for Point 4

Sigil for Point 9

Sigil for Point 5

Sigil for Point 10

The Goddess Archetypes

1. ***Michba-huresvi – (Panatura)*** – *She who breathes life into dreams.*

Fertility and rapid manifestation result from the co-operative creativity of the masculine and feminine; the combination of quality and quantity, activity within rest.

2. ***Viresva-ashana – (Ama-terra-su)*** – *She who gathers gems of inspiration.*

The past remains as part of the present as its inspiration. This creates inspired living.

3. **Belspa-mivechvi – (Ka-li-ma)** – *She who parts the veils.*

The law of compensation creates a circular movement, like a dog chasing its tail, within physicality, since something is always owed. In recognizing indivisible fullness, life becomes still.

4. **Kresna-haraspi – (Ori-ka-la)** – *She who hears the Eternal Song.*

The feminine realms lie outside the physical cosmos the way a Nagual's double luminous cocoon overlap each other. They are both dream bodies. To know the song of the dreamer, is to know future trends.

5. *Bivinet-ashi – (Au-ba-ri)* – *She who restores dynamic balance through adjusting emphasis.*

The knowledge that we change the outer world by adjusting the one within, is represented by this archetype.

6. *Meresh-arestu – (Hay-hu-ka)* – *She who embraces spontaneous experience.*

The masculine illusion that there is a need to accumulate knowledge rather than joyfully experience unfolding life, is dissolved by spontaneous living.

7. *Nichtararech-usvi – (Ishana-ma)* – *She who lives the poetic perspective.*

The graceful elegance of becoming an unfolding work of art, is embodied by this archetype.

8. *Avaresvi-hurarat – (Aparatura)* – *She who knows change through alternating emphasis.*

The illusion that something is gone because its contribution is less emphasized, is replaced by an endless perspective.

9. **Meshrut-araveshbavi – (Hay-leem-a)** – *She who knows the bounty of limitless supply.*

Not holding on to present manifestations, but knowing ourselves to be conduits of everlasting supply, we become one with abundant life.

10. **Nura-ustami – (Uru-ama)** – *She who embraces the inspiration of creative flow.*

The eternal part of us is the creative dreamer and life and death our works of art.

11. *Nuch-ret-eresvi* – *(Amaraku)* – *She who has found the innocence of un-self-conscious living.*

Life can be renewing, or death can be allowed to erode life away. For it to be renewed, we must be free of self-reflection.

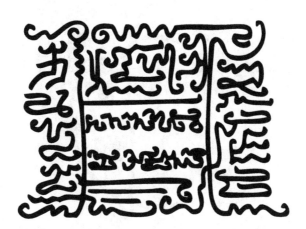

12. *Neshet-viraspi-heresha* – *(Alu-mi-na)* – *She who embraces the impure within the pure.*

The rejecting of the 'impure,' is a judgment of the heart that strengthens it. Allowing the impure to pass through the pure, like wind through the trees, cancels it out.

The God Archetypes

1. *Chechmet-va-urvaset (La-u-mi-el)* – *Lord of inclusiveness*

This archetype closes the gap between cause and effect, which is the essential meaning of white magic. In closing the gap between giving and receiving and other polar opposites, the density of life decreases.

2. *Barakruvael (Akasha-el)* – *Lord of inspiration*

Akashic records are held in place during past cycles of life by 'ghosts of the past' that refuse to evolve as life moves to higher consciousness. This archetype releases attachments to the past by incorporating them into the present as inspiration for change or accomplishment.

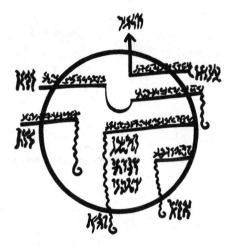

3. *Breshbranuch-aravat (Karama)* – *Lord of the clearing of karma*

Karma is deliberately created by life and death so that awareness is called back to their realms. The body, which uses the tool of life, deliberately creates blind spots that obscure the proper motivation for our actions. The soul deliberately gives bad advice as we call upon our higher self so as to create emotional turmoil – creating karma in the soul world we pass to after death. Unfulfilled karma has been the lure of the soul and the body to perpetuate its cycles of existence. This archetype helps see behind the appearances that obscure clear vision so as to eliminate karma and thereby the tyranny of life and death.

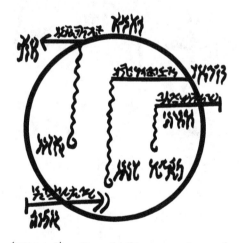

4. *Mishbech-brach-stanavik (Uri-el)* – *Lord of integration of opposites*

The mind chooses through intelligence; the heart chooses through sentimental value – both are based on judgment. This creates egocentricity as the little self tries to decide what should and shouldn't be. In a life surrendered to the orchestration of the Infinite One there is no personal choice other than the excellence with which you perform the inevitable. This archetype replaces judgment with inspired excellence.

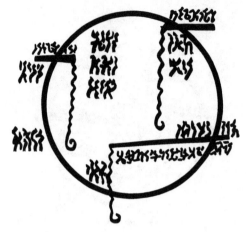

5. *Briach-bresh-veset (Ki-as-mus)* – *Lord that clears inertia*

When it is time for the veils of illusion that form the incubation chambers of life to release, it can either be done through forced change or through the gentle promptings of the dance. He promotes inspired change through promptings of rapture, passion and joy, rather than through the painful change that is forced upon us.

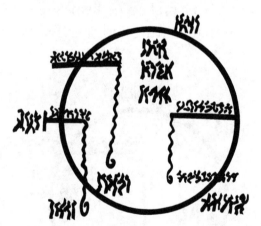

6. *Bishbarach-nuvaset (Mira-el)* – *Lord of the adventure of the journey*

This archetype promotes the knowledge that nothing is hidden. We hide portions of existence from ourselves simply by contracting our focus either to promote the appreciation of the details or as a means of guiding us into a new direction. He promotes perception that eliminates the llusion of victimhood.

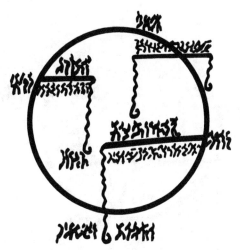

7. *Brishparauf-braset (Om-ka-el)* – *Lord who holds the vision*

This archetype combines fluidity with vision. He instills the knowledge that all foreseen possibilities are but a fluid starting point of excellence beyond the imagining. Genius and exceptional accomplishments cannot be foreseen within existing paradigms – this is the principle this archetype represents.

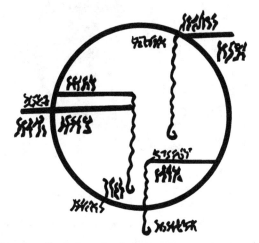

8. *Avarentura-misha-el (Kapa-el)* – *Lord of the cycles*

This archetype uses the simultaneous expression of opposites in a dance of mutual inspiration to eliminate linear change. He facilitates the ability to know the eternal, indivisible intent of the Infinite.

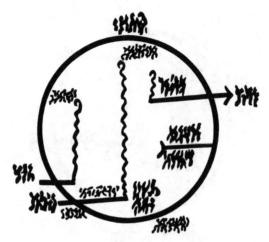

9. *Vraba-usvaset-nichta (Leemu-el)* – *Lord of the flow of awareness*

He encourages the removal of resistance to the inevitable flow of existence, thereby stopping the movement of time. He promotes the purity of life through timelessness.

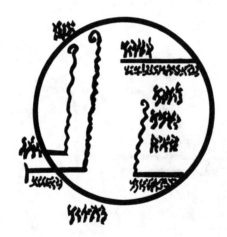

10. *Vira-utret-unama (Iluminati)* – *Lord of illumination*

This archetype knows the flow of fluid structure through being the messenger of foreseeing Infinite Intent. He is also called the messenger of the Mother.

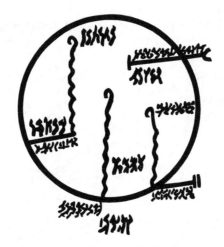

11. *Pretprak-paravur-vileshta (Kumara)* – *Lord of hierarchy and government*

This archetype carries the knowledge that in the surrendered life the only part that can be governed is the quality of one's response to that which is unfolding. This affects the quality of the environment. Change is exponential and graceful when the little egoic self surrenders to Infinite's Intent.

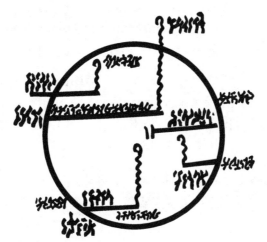

12. *Trechba-uvrasbi-hurastat (Ka-li-sa)* – *Lord of energy distribution*

This archetype is also known as the divine lover. He is the one that surrenders to his divine counterpart in unconditional love. He is the bringer of resurrection as the body embraces the soul.

Q. Why is the physical shape the way that it is? Are there other dominant shapes throughout the cosmos?

A. The human form is the predominant shape. Angels, demons, and star people are all, more or less, the same shape because of two reasons:

1. The embodiment of the Infinite is the original template that is the determinative shape as waves of creation are expressed in fractal, repetitive patterns.

2. Secondly, it is a design carved by countless eons of expressed individuations (each person's experiences within the Infinite's Intent, shaping form, like a river carves a rock formation as it flows through the ages, each drop contributing).

Q. Why are the body and nature connected? How does this happen?

A. In the *Lemurian Science of Immortality,* it is written: "What are the flesh and the material world but a program that is temporarily imagined within the Infinite Being?" So, you see, the body and Nature are part of the same program, derived from the same original fractal template.

Q. In the *Lemurian Science of Immortality,* you write: "Fear of loss of the flesh keeps the illusion of material life in place. Gross is the environment that is made from the coarseness of matter." Doesn't that tell us that the material body is unworthy as a tool?

A. Well, the next sentence after your quote says: "Honor the body but eliminate the flesh – the program that binds life into contraction. When the program of matter dissolves, pristiness remains." The sentence after that tells you how to "eliminate the flesh".

> "The eternal can dissolve the unreal by seeing that it has never existed,
> matter has never in reality existed. Remove it by knowing this."

It invites you to look beyond the appearance of form and the tyranny of flesh so that eternal matter, or spiritualized matter, can reveal itself.

Q. Is this the way to achieve immortality, to delay the decay of the flesh?

A. To delay the decay of flesh, and to prolong life, is no more valuable than to delay rebirth by prolonging death. Both are seen as meaningless when we enter into the timelessness of the eternal nature of our being.

*Weave your dreams and hopes into realities
from the river of the starry skies that flow
through the endlessness of your being.*

Discourse 4
Prayer, Ceremony and Ritual

Q. There are such differences in the ways that people pray. Which one is correct?

A. Spiritual maturity (our relationship with Source and our expression in our environment) evolves through different stages as life awakens in consciousness. Each stage relates differently to its Source through prayer.

Q. What are these stages of evolving spiritual maturity?

A. Dependence: this can be found in religious fanatics, where religion has become a dependency, like a drug that dominates their life.

The second stage is co-dependence. This is the stage where most religious people are. They bargain with god, "If I do this, then will you bless me with that?" They try and control outcome through prayer when problems arise – but when all is well, their religion is pushed in the background.

Q. Many people have become repulsed by their infantile and subservient role to religious leaders and have turned their back on religion. What about them?

A. They are part of a growing trend, forerunners of the next evolutionary stage of independence.

Q. These three groups seem to make up the majority of the population, like the broad base of the pyramid. What are the next stages?

A. The next stage, interdependence is based on mind expansion through broadening vision.

Q. Give an example please.

A. Let's say there's something in your life that you don't like. Previously, you would have asked the Infinite to change it. Now, you change your reality by seeing things you've never seen before, using the adversity as an indicator as to where to examine deeper understanding and new observations. You self govern the quality of your life by changing how you look at things. This interdependence stage can be called the young adult level of spiritual development. It is the first stage in which the individual takes accountability and responsibility for their reality.

Q. So how does prayer look for these people?

A. It is a request for clarity: "What blind spot in me created this situation, and what must I see to uncreate it?" This is asked of the One expressing as the many, and the person then watches for the answer, which may express as effortless knowing or from signs in the environment.

Q. Where does the evidence of the heart come in?

A. In the next stage, the stage of autonomy or one-heartedness. The heart asks the prayerful question: "Which part of life do I separate myself from through judgment, which part do I exclude from my compassionate understanding?" In this way, we change our reality by changing our attitude to one of acceptance.

Q. You have not really mentioned following the promptings of the heart?

A. No, because the generally accepted idea of following one's heart is grossly misunderstood. The heart does provide clues of where our exclusiveness has produced adversity, but its promptings for most are need based. Its emotions spring from desires to be fulfilled, and as a source of guidance, it is tainted.

Q. Is there no other source of guidance from the heart?

A. Yes, the visceral response of all our organs, (tightening of the stomach, tightness of the lungs, etc.) gives us non-cognitive information about our environment.

Q. What would be the sixth stage of spiritual guidance?

A. One-heartedness and one-mindedness combine in the stage of self-sovereignty. In this stage the person's heart is open as they approach life with the true meaning of intimacy: leading with an opened heart. They feel the subtle nuances of the currents of life steer them, and they fully cooperate, while their vision maintains an eternal, timeless perspective with attention to the details (the signs of the environment speaking to them).

Q. Do personal desires cease at this point?

A. Yes, they become fluid preferences as the person's life starts to unfold with graceful support. The prayers become prayers of acknowledgment and gratitude. The person brings increase to certain areas of their life through the accentuation of gratitude. The menace of an attitude of victimization starts to dramatically diminish.

THE EMOTIONS OF RECOGNITION

1a	*Plenitude*	The recognition that I have all
1b	*Omni-presence*	The recognition that I am all
2a	*Rapture*	The recognition of Infinite existence in stillness
2b	*Reverential Existence*	The recognition of Mundane Sacredness
3a	*Omni-perspective*	The recognition of simplicity in complexity
3b	*Timelessness*	The recognition of the fullness of all in the moment
4a	*Creating Absolute Truth*	The recognition of existence as a devotional prayer
4b	*Fulfilled Contentment*	The recognition of the unfolding wonderment of existence
5a	*Awakened Awareness*	The recognition of meticulous caring
5b	*Fluid Vastness*	The recognition of dynamic balance in expression
6a	*Supported Expression*	The recognition of limitless supply of resources
6b	*Deep Peace*	The recognition of the self as the only being in existence
7a	*Effortless Knowing*	The recognition of indivisible existence
7b	*Unchangeable Perfection*	The recognition of new revelations
8a	*Carefree Surrender*	The recognition of the impeccability of timing of the unfolding revelations of Oneness
8b	*Harmonic Resonance*	The recognition of the perfection of expressions of diverse consciousness
9a	*Lighthearted Eternal Presence*	The recognition of fluid, eternal existence
9b	*Comforting Presence*	The recognition of floating on the calm waves of existence
10a	*Perpetual Freshness of Expression*	The recognition of countless possibilities of eternal existence
10b	*Eternal Fulfillment*	The recognition of the complete equity of existence
11a	*Supreme Elegance*	The recognition of infinite diversity of beauty
11b	*Confidence of Purity*	The recognition of the benevolence of unfolding life
12a	*Humorous Conjunction*	The recognition of Infinite bliss
12b	*Transient Expression of Indivisible Form*	The recognition of form as the ever-renewed vehicle of Infinite Intent

THE 12 PURE PAIRS OF EMOTIONS

	(-)	(+)
1	**Trust**	**Love**
	The desire to surrender (replaced fear)	The desire to include
2	**Peace**	**Inspiration**
	The desire to be at ease, to feel at home (replaced protectiveness)	The desire to inspire and to be inspired (replaced anger)
3	**Pleasure**	**Creativity**
	The desire to be delighted	The desire to create
4	**Acknowledgement**	**Empathy**
	The desire to see perfection	The desire to connect
5	**Receptivity**	**Generosity**
	The desire to receive	The desire to give
6	**Beauty**	**Encouragement**
	The desire to be uplifted	The desire to encourage and to be encouraged
7	**Assimilation**	**Communication**
	The desire to integrate	The desire to express
8	**Joy**	**Passion**
	The desire to live	The desire to know
9	**Fun**	**Achievement**
	The desire to revel	The desire to excel
10	**Contentment**	**Enlightenment**
	The desire to retain (replaced pain)	The desire to enhance and to to be enhanced
11	**Humor**	**Empowerment**
	The desire to be amused	The desire to be of service
12	**Satisfaction**	**Growth**
	The desire to be fulfilled	The desire to expand

Q. This seems to be the first stage of 'the glass is half full' perspective.

A. Exactly. The seventh stage is the stage of absolute oneness. This stage has a lot of automatic action, coupled with increased abilities to feel the guidance of the inner senses (see the *Book of Runes*). The borders between what is spiritual and what is not diminishes, and our prayer becomes our response of praise to the wonders of life.

Q. Are there only 7 stages?

A. No, there are eight. These last three are generally found in resurrected beings.

Q. What can you tell us about the eighth?

A. It is fully empathic and telepathic. It becomes impossible to watch violence on television for instance; one feels it as though it is inside them. The fully empathic, telepathic state comes from the resurrected (3rd stage) master's ability to live from inner and outer space (called bilaterality and directionality) at once.

Q. How is this done?

A. By opening the High Heart in the sternum as a result of absolute trust in your self-support developed in the previous stage. Here your life is guided by inspiration that ripples through the cells. You become the prayer as you respond to the promptings of the Infinite in the form of inspiration.

Q. What is ceremony, and what is its value assuming that it has some?

A. Ceremony is a specific organizing of events in our environment. By that I mean it is a way of designing our environment to affect our attitude and worldview.

Q. Give an example please?

A. We design something to create a specific focus, and to create importance for a specific event. One can take a bath at night, scrub behind the ears, and be done. Or you can make it a bathing ceremony with candles, ambient music and alchemical oils in order to signal to the brain to approach the event with reverence, so that you can wash away the debris of the day, not just the dirt. Through ceremony, something ordinary is turned into something extraordinary. You have created a high point in your day.

Q. What is ritual?

A. A ritual on the other hand, focuses intent, directs vision and draws power for a specific outcome.

Q. Isn't it black magic to enforce our will on the environment?

A. Not if we change our environment by changing ourselves. As co-creators of our reality, which we are at the high levels of maturity, we may intend a general outcome, but allow the Infinite to design the specifics of how it is fulfilled in a way that benefits all involved.

Q. How does this work?

A. The dynamics are that the ritual creates a stage where the intent behind the ritual can be fulfilled. The Infinite then directs a play upon the stage in keeping with our general intent.

Q. The stage is a new reality that's created?

A. No, it's a designated space within a reality, where a specific focus is being articulated. So, you will notice that the many rituals we've received upon this sacred journey have always been have accompanied by life-altering insights, and the internalizing of certain insights and attributes by the practitioner that change the practitioner as well as effecting change in our environment. These insights aren't just any insights, but ones that are specifically designed to release the power of the particular ritual.

Q. What is a typical anatomy of a ritual?

A. The changing of the practitioner evolves the awareness, and in doing so, releases the power that was tied up by the previous illusions that were held in the lower level of awareness. The practitioner's shift provides a power source for the ritual, directed by the practitioner's intent.

Q. Is that the main power source?

A. It is a primary power source, but also a catalyst that unlocks the resources of a second power source: the sacred wheels and sigils, and sometimes the alchemical equations used in the ritual.

Q. What makes the wheels sacred?

A. A good word, often misused to mean important: they are sacred because they are living entities that contain awareness. They are sacred because they are capable of shifting awareness every time cosmic awareness evolves. They strengthen anyone using them, as evidenced by muscle testing, because they were given by the Infinite. Their patterns represent certain aspects of the creational grid that is an expression of the Infinite.

Q. It is said that you've stopping including student's sigils and wheels in your books because it causes the book to muscle test weakly?

A. That's correct. Those wheels are for their personal use. The ones from the Infinite are for the entire world. I learned the hard way after having to pull a book off the market, not long after publishing it.

The Ceremony of Rejuvenation

Esklavanit Verevusta

THE PROGRAM FOR CLAIMING THE DIVINE
HERITAGE OF TIMELESSNESS

The cause of aging and disease in the body is linear time. Linear time comes from resistance to life. Timelessness, the divine heritage of man, comes from surrender

Esklavanit

The program is divided into two sections:

a) The protocol for the body

b) The protocol for the face.

They can be done separately or together. When doing them together, follow the protocol for the body first and then the face. Use meditative background music. (The Sacred Breaths of Arasatma sound elixir MP3 download is provided with this book.)

Step 1

The Anointing (This is optional, but recommended.)

Anoint the 13 joints of the body as shown with lotus oil – or instruct your client how to do this. You may assist your client if you are appropriately licensed to do so.

Anoint the head with rose oil in preparation for the face protocol. Use the sigils as instructed for the 13 joints of the head.

Step 2

The Program for Clearing the Body and Face

Position: Lying on the back with legs straight and arms relaxed at sides.

Place the Wheel that Dissolves Old Programs of Guilt and Unworthiness a few inches above the head.

The Tablets for Dissolving Old Programs of Guilt and Unworthiness are placed in a stack a few inches below the feet (number 1 is on the top, number 26 is at the bottom). Have a list of the names of the tablets available to read during ceremony.

Start the ceremony by reading the name of the first tablet on the list. Visualize the tablet moving up through the body as you simultaneously sweep your hands from the feet to the top of the head (1 inch above the body, without touching it). Shake your hands above the Wheel that Dissolves Old Programs of Guilt and Unworthiness as though you are shaking the density you have just removed from their body into the Wheel. Visualize the tablet that has moved through the body, also going into the wheel (the physical stack of tablets remains at the feet).

Continue in exactly the same way as you visualize the remaining 25 tablets moving through the body.

Note: Step 2 is the same whether doing the body, the face or both. Remove the wheel and tablets after completing Step 2.

Step 3
The Program for Establishing Timelessness in the Body and Face

The 26 Tablets of Claiming the Divine Heritage each have an accompanying attitude. Attitudes 1 – 13 for Claiming the Divine Heritage are for establishing timelessness in the body. Attitudes 14-26 are for establishing timelessness in the face.

If doing the protocol for the body only, place Tablets 1 – 13 for the Attitudes on the Power Wheel for Claiming the Divine Heritage. If using only the protocol for the face, place Tablets 14 – 26 for the Attitudes on the Power Wheel. When using the protocols for the face and the body, use all 26 Tablets. The lowest number is always placed on top of the stack and the highest number at the bottom.

Place Power Wheel for Claiming the Divine Heritage with the appropriate stack of Tablets on top of it below the feet. Have a list of the Attitudes close by so that you can read them during the ceremony.

Begin by reading the first Attitude of Claiming the Divine Heritage (reading the sacred language is optional).

Envision the first tablet moving up through the body while deeply considering the meaning of the attitude and what it would be like to embody it. When working with a client, it is important that they also contemplate this.

Continue in this way with each successive tablet, until you have integrated all the attitudes and envisioned all the tablets having moved through the body (the physical stack remains at the feet).

Now, envision the Power Wheel moving up through the body, from the bottom of the feet and out through the top of the head.

While the Power Wheel is moving through, the body should be completely relaxed. If you (or your client) feel any areas of tension or resistance, breath deeply, exhaling the tension out of the body, until it has all been released. (Tension may be remnants of resistance that hold linear time in the body.)

Close the ceremony by saying the following:

Nesh karavet hurspata eres visach bravabit ereklu.

I am a timeless expression of infinite glory.

Remain in meditation for a short while. Remove the Power Wheel and Tablets after completing Step 3.

Anointing the 13 Joints and Head

Using *Lotus Oil*, place a small drop, rubbing it lightly for a few seconds in a clockwise manner, on the front of the each of the joints as follows:

Ankles

Knees

Hip joints

Both wrists – on the back of the hand where the forearm and the hand meet

Both elbows – on the outside of the arm

Both shoulders – at the top of the arm where it meets the shoulder

Under the chin – where the skull and the neck meet, above the larynx

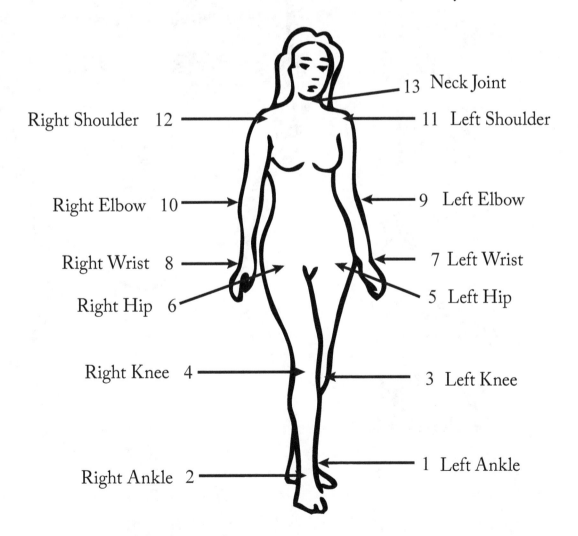

Right Shoulder 12 — — 13 Neck Joint — 11 Left Shoulder

Right Elbow 10 — — 9 Left Elbow

Right Wrist 8 — — 7 Left Wrist

Right Hip 6 — — 5 Left Hip

Right Knee 4 — — 3 Left Knee

Right Ankle 2 — — 1 Left Ankle

Apply one drop of *Rose Oil* to each of 13 points indicated on the face and the back of the head. As you apply the oil, either look at the relevant sigil for that point, or run your index finger from left to right over the sigil. You may use the index finger of either hand.

Sigil for Point 1

Sigil for Point 2

Sigil for Point 3

Sigil for Point 4

Sigil for Point 5

Sigil for Point 6

Sigil for Point 7

Sigil for Point 8

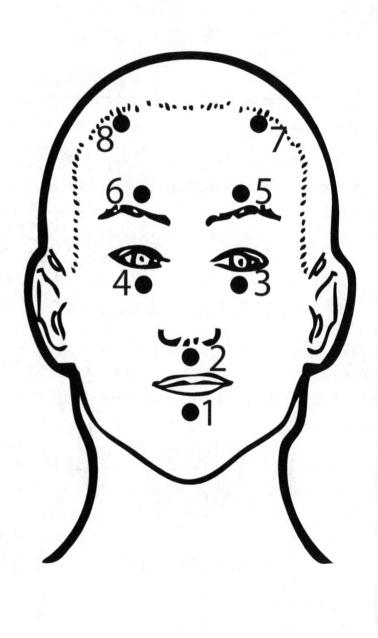

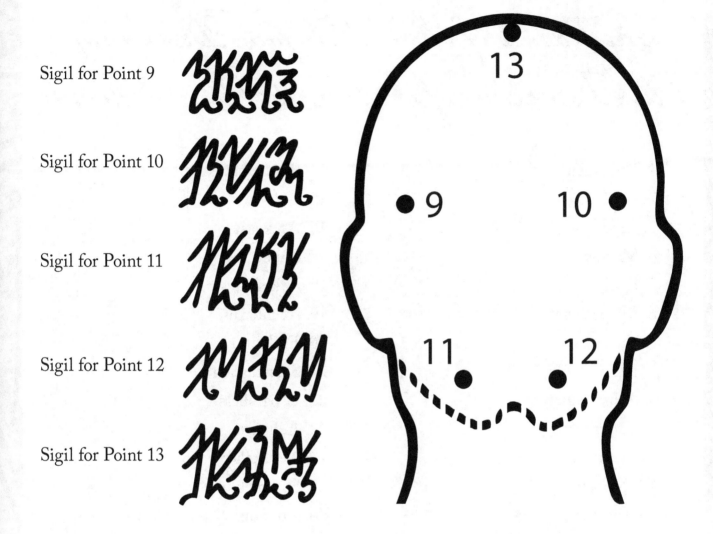

Sigil for Point 9

Sigil for Point 10

Sigil for Point 11

Sigil for Point 12

Sigil for Point 13

The Names of the Tablets for Dissolving Old Programs of Guilt and Unworthiness

1. Nuhasach
2. Petrivu
3. Kilsater
4. Menevu
5. Kruhasat
6. Mispechvi
7. Huspater
8. Erekvi
9. Achstuvahet
10. Brivachspi
11. Mesetur
12. Nananes
13. Elsuvater
14. Skruhabaves
15. Neksutar
16. Arekvastahur
17. Blihevaset
18. Arkbivares
19. Nechbarus
20. Ereklatvi
21. Sarsaranach
22. Usbaranek
23. Achparu
24. Nenskelvat
25. Sutbereklut
26. Minahur

Tablets for Dissolving Old Programs of Guilt and Unworthiness

Tablet 1. *Nuhasach*

Tablet 2. *Petrivu*

Tablet 3. *Kilsater*

Tablet 4. *Menevu*

Tablet 5. *Kruhasat*

Tablet 6. *Mispechvi*

Tablet 7. *Huspater*

Tablet 8. *Erekvi*

Tablet 9. *Achstuvahet*

Tablet 10. *Brivachspi*

Tablet 11. *Mesetur*

Tablet 12. *Nananes*

Tablet 13. *Elsuvater*

Tablet 14. *Skruhabaves*

Tablet 15. *Neksutar*

Tablet 16. *Arekvastahur*

Tablet 17. *Blihevaset*

Tablet 18. *Arkbivares*

Tablet 19. *Nechbarus*

Tablet 20. *Ereklatvi*

Tablet 21. *Sarsaranach*

Tablet 22. *Usbaranek*

Tablet 23. *Achparu*

Tablet 24. *Nenskelvat*

84

Tablet 25. *Sutbereklut*   Tablet 26. *Minahur*

The Attitudes of Claiming the Divine Heritage Tablets

Tablet 1

Mechpe herusit arachva menunish
I am a luminous and divine miracle

Tablet 2

Keresta huhechvi menusat velevish
Freedom from the tyranny of opposites

Tablet 3

Sihet iskletvi heruhich ustatve
Unified fields of perception

Tablet 4

Karsanut mitruvech serasut uvechvi
Living beyond distorted emotions

Tablet 5

Nerek satve menunech suvatvi
Boundlessness as a constant expectation

Tablet 6

Istererek misetret usaba vetvi
Willingness to shine in excellence

Tablet 7

Skarachvi nestararut sivrehet
The rich fullness of divinity in action

Tablet 8

Nechpa heres eresta menuvich ersat vibrech haresta
Willingness to ascend beyond the paradigm of the masses

Tablet 9

Kirsata menes eresta haruhit
The release of inner tension

Tablet 10

Sihech ersklatvrava herat ersetu
The Bliss of Remembered Innocence

Tablet 11

Kishach herestu minaves esekle hurasvi aresta
Embracing the eternal state of worthiness

Tablet 12

Pihech estereva mines arasva herset minuch esta minavit
The sovereignty of choosing the quality of the never-ending journey

Tablet 13

Esekle mirat bivech sersavat arek binavit klivesvi
sihech plihavis enesve
Releasing ages of feeling displaced by finding the home
within

Tablet 14

Sivanich ereta kluhis misachve nenuhit arsta privanech
selvenut hursta
Creating heaven on Earth through the attitude of delighted
appreciation

Tablet 15

Kesech mesta enuhit sevach vibrestu
The endless companion of deep peace

Tablet 16

Askahet sevech viherestu manahit
The glow of self-fulfillment

Tablet 17

Keseta eresatva mistenut karanes esklevit harasvi miseta
The comforting presence of the abiding connection with the Earth

Tablet 18

Nesech isetu klavis vibret mines eresu harstat
Cradled by the support of all existence

Tablet 19

Privech sechsevi erasta misevet ekletvi virasech
Surges of gladness over acknowledged blessings

Tablet 20

Karsat erestava minech sersava kravanes usta
Relaxed mastery of the manipulation of time

Tablet 21

Sersata kihuranes mivet arsklahut meneset
The joyous recognition of being timeless

Tablet 22

Kares hesetu mistavit erachve miset ukles haverestu
Living from the sovereignty of your chosen reality

Tablet 23

Kisana hesatu skivelvas anasta
The blessed release of density

Tablet 24

Kavanet eskelvi brivach harsat menestu avesvi
Appreciating the graceful home of your body

Tablet 25

Kahanesh estu mivach haresta privatur mistet kelesta
Existing beyond the opposites of age and youth

Tablet 26

Meskenach hurspa kereverenat sarsatu huvesvi aklat
The rapture of the adventure of individuation

The Attitudes of Claiming the Divine Heritage

1. Mechpe herusit arachva menunish
I am a luminous and divine miracle

2. Keresta huhechvi menusat velevish
Freedom from the tyranny of opposites

3. Sihet iskletvi heruhich ustatve
Unified fields of perception

4. Karsanut mitruvech serasut uvechvi
Living beyond distorted emotions

5. Nerek satve menunech suvatvi
Boundlessness as a constant expectation

6. Istererek misetret usaba vetvi
Willingness to shine in excellence

7. Skarachvi nestararut sivrehet
The rich fullness of divinity in action

8. Nechpa heres eresta menuvich ersat vibrech haresta
Willingness to ascend beyond the paradigm of the masses

9. Kirsata menes eresta haruhit
The release of inner tension

10. Sihech ersklatvrava herat ersetu
The Bliss of Remembered Innocence

11. Kishach herestu minaves esekle hurasvi aresta
Embracing the eternal state of worthiness

12. Pihech estereva mines arasva herset minuch esta minavit
The sovereignty of choosing the quality of the never-ending journey

13. Esekle mirat bivech sersavat arek binavit klivesvi sihech plihavis enesve
Releasing ages of feeling displaced by finding the home within

14. Sivanich ereta kluhis misachve nenuhit arsta privanech selvenut hursta
Creating heaven on Earth through the attitude of delighted appreciation

15. Kesech mesta enuhit sevach vibrestu
The endless companion of deep peace

16. Askahet sevech viherestu manahit
The glow of self-fulfillment

17. Keseta eresatva mistenut karanes esklevit harasvi miseta
The comforting presence of the abiding connection with the Earth

18. Nesech isetu klavis vibret mines eresu harstat
Cradled by the support of all existence

19. Privech sechsevi erasta misevet ekletvi virasech
Surges of gladness over acknowledged blessings

20. Karsat erestava minech sersava kravanes usta
Relaxed mastery of the manipulation of time

21. Sersata kihuranes mivet arsklahut meneset
The joyous recognition of being timeless

22. Kares hesetu mistavit erachve miset ukles haverestu
Living from the sovereignty of your chosen reality

23. Kisana hesatu skivelvas anasta
The blessed release of density

24. Kavanet eskelvi brivach harsat menestu avesvi
Appreciating the graceful home of your body

25. Kahanesh estu mivach haresta privatur mistet kelesta
Existing beyond the opposites of age and youth

26. Meskenach hurspa kereverenat sarsatu huvesvi aklat
The rapture of the adventure of individuation

Discourse 5
Principles of Regeneration and Rejuvenation

Q. Please clarify the differences between regeneration and rejuvenation.

A. Both have to do with altering cellular programming and changing the frequency of the cells. It can be said that both are based on the renewal of cells but that rejuvenation has an extra step: replacing the old program with a specific new one. The memory of the cell of being say, 70 years old, is altered to think of itself as say, 20 years old.

Q. But isn't that a lie that we're instilling into our cells?

A. Well, since we're eternal and timeless, claiming to be 70 years old is a lie. But I agree with you: Programming any age into our cells is an illusion upon the eternal stage of our existence. Whereas, embracing timelessness is really the goal, not youth or maturity.

Q. But renewing cells is surely a good thing?

A. All cells in our body renew themselves automatically every seven years. It is said by some scientists that blood cells renew themselves every seven days. So everyone is never older than seven years before their cells are rebirthing.

Q. Then why do some age? I should really say, why do 'most' age?

A. Because the automatic cellular renewing gets interrupted by the collective belief systems of aging, decay and death.

Q. At what age does this interruption begin?

A. Normally, by age 11.

Q. That's so early!

A. Yes, the mental enslavement of parental and environmental social conditioning is very entrenched by age 12, which is the reason teenagers rebel to try and find their own authenticity.

Q. You have a 16-year old adopted daughter, how rebellious is she?

A. Not at all. I receive nothing but love and respect from her! She is a joy to raise.

Q. How many of your teachings, sought after by worldwide audiences, have you given to her?

A. I've not shared one of my teachings with her except to answer her questions occasionally. If there's something she wishes to learn from me, it will have to be through example. I approach her with humility that I may learn from her, and try to provide her with the shelter of a home that's heaven on Earth, so that her unique greatness can grow and flourish.

Q. It is said that the ancient Egyptians had a way to regenerate and youthen the body. Can you teach us that?

A. They used black magic, so the answer is no, I cannot teach you that.

Q. You have defined black magic as that which tries to enforce its will on outcome, and also that which enhances itself by diminishing someone else. Isn't an attempt to make the body believe it's 20 years old (rejuvenation) a way of trying to control outcome?

A. There are degrees of black magic, and the resulting karmic repercussions. The most severe black magic tries to injure or bind another. The other very severe form is to take from another to enhance yourself. The next is to try and enforce your will onto others, and onto an outcome.

Q. It sounds as if social conditioning could fall into this category…

A. It does. The Egyptians used the 2nd form of sever black magic and when the knowledge of how to do these practices was lost they started mummifying their bodies for the time that the black magic would again be remembered.

Q. So there's nothing we can learn from them…?

A. To the contrary. Black magic often contains principles that have long since been forgotten by masters in other traditions, and that can be applied in an impeccable way that benefits all life.

Q. Please explain.

A. The Egyptians stole life force and energetic resources from disincarnate beings in the soul world, the dead. This lowered the life force in some of them so much that they sank into the underworld, captured by their own lack of consciousness. High consciousness requires high levels of available resources.

Q. What can we learn from this?

A. That additional power and resources are needed for cellular regeneration. We achieve this by increasing perception. Hence, we provide life-altering insights with our rituals. When I see the life force they stole, it looks like a grey fabric that they wrapped the recipient in (mummy style). Power released by perception glows with white light from within the person, because it is so much purer.

Q. What else did they use?

A. Electric surges, like those obtained from electric eels. The purpose was to wipe the memory of age clean from the cells, the same way an electric surge can wipe a computer's memory clean.

Q. What can we do to clear memories of aging from our cells?

A. The old memories are held in the frequencies of the cells – the same way the magnetic component of the tape in a tape recorder holds the memory of the music you recorded. You can change that memory by replacing it with a new frequency. The new frequency is created in several ways: Enhanced perception creates enhanced frequencies, this journey has provided ample opportunities for increased perception and students have reported spontaneous youthening. Secondly, we've been given specific techniques to evolve our DNA through the use of the Runes (see *Book of Runes*) and the Magic of the Gods (see *Entering Godhood* online course, part 1-3). An advanced DNA system, when articulated in our lives through living the principles the DNA chambers represent, will reprogram the cells into incorruptibility.

Q. What else was a component that they used in their ritual?

A. The last component was that they surrounded the recipient with 16 people who would use subtle suggestion, who would verbally program and visualize the person as young. In this way they would create a new personal matrix for the person. A matrix is held in place by geometry. All this would take place in a pyramid.

Q. What does this teach us?

A. It teaches us what not to do. Any matrix, personal or otherwise, captures the awareness. Any reality held in place by a matrix cannot endure forever and must eventually break down – a bit like Cinderella at midnight when her coach turned back into a pumpkin and her ball gown turned to rags.

THE DNA ROSE OF AN ENLIGHTENED BEING
- CONTAINS 441 PETALS

THE DNA ROSE OF A RESURRECTED BEING
- CONTAINS 672 PETALS

Q. What is the significance of number 16 – 8 women and 8 men, I presume?

A. Correct. A reality held in place by a geometric matrix, creates a space that differentiates itself by its specific qualities (the life force of a 20-year old for instance). To form a space, we need to have eight directions. Since we're not aiming to have a matrix: a programmed, conditioned life, we have to dissolve previous matrices. We have to dissolve the illusions that keep the eight directions in place (see the *Bridge of No Time*).

Q. But 8 directions aren't 16. How did they arrive at the number 16?

A. Each direction has two poles – a masculine and a feminine – an active and passive element. If we receive the perceptions to replace the illusions that keep the directions in place, the directions will disappear, and with them, the matrices that they keep in place.

Sweep now space, for sacred it is
The benevolent playground of the Holy One
Almine

The Magic of the Gods
Perpetual Regeneration Ceremony

THE THIRD-RING MAGIC OF THE GODS

- First ring magic uses external sources and allies to effect changes in reality.

- Second ring magic changes the world by changing within.

- Third ring magic uses integrated cooperation between inner realities and external allies to create outer circumstances through inner emphases.

The DNA strand of a god-being has 300 strands, or frequency chambers, in the first and second levels of godhood, and 441 DNA strands in the third level of godhood. This represents the 441 frequency components of the cosmos. Cosmic events can be orchestrated by emphasizing certain corresponding chambers within the DNA. This is the basis for third ring magic: *Magic Through Emphases* — The Magic of the Gods.

The external allies that are used are the 441 angel gods that preside over the cosmic frequency chambers. Their assignments are encoded in letter and number combinations, and different templates are used for different purposes. A specific DNA chamber (or 'petal') may have one letter / number combination for the magic of self-regeneration of the cells, and another for the magic of successful business.

Each magical purpose has a specific number of principles. Each principle has a sigil, and five angel gods that respond to that sigil.

Each principle's five angels (each with its own code) are involved in drawing that principle's sigil. This is done until all sigils for all principles (30, in the case of the magic for the regeneration of the cells) are complete.

HOW TO PREPARE FOR THE MAGICAL CEREMONY

You will need 30 copies of the blank template. (See the front of this book to access the pdf and MP3 downloads). Alternatively can can use pre-drawn sigils, in which case you will trace them with your finger.

Note: The numbers in parentheses are given only for creating the sigils, they are not used in the ceremony.

Each sigil has angel names, codes and numbers, similar to the following:

- (16) Erseta – **ST11**
- (84) Ururuk – **49ST**
- (124) Hesetu – **69L**
- (8) Prihanit – **FBDX**
- (438) Eseklet-nisar – **TLPC**

The above names and codes are for the drawing and use of the first principle for cellular regeneration. The rose code template enables you to identify the petals and their codes.

The sigil is drawn on a numbered rose template (a transparency is recommended). Draw a little circle on petal 16 on the blank template. Draw a straight line from there to petal 84, then to 124, and on to 8. From 8, draw a straight line to 438, and from there to the center of the rose, where the line ends in a little circle. All sigils start with a little circle on the first petal mentioned, and end with a little circle in the middle of the numbered rose.

Place the sigil's template face down on the table next to you, and continue creating the other 29 sigils, placing the numbered sigils up-side down on top of the first one. You are creating a stack of 30 sigils, with the first on top and the 30th one on the bottom when you turn the stack over.

Line up all the stars on the pages with the 30 sigils. Place on top of and line them up with the rose template containing the codes. Place this stack on top of the DNA rose, aligning all the stars. Clip them together so they do not get displaced – the proper alignment is very important.

Say the following incantation:
Trehach menuset arasta

Place the stack below your feet as you lie on your back. You will no longer be needing the blank template with the numbers (if you used a blank template to create sigils on transparencies).

01 *Self-sustaining emotional self-sovereignty*

(16) Erseta – **ST11**
(84) Ururuk – **49ST**
(124) Hesetu – **69L**
(8) Prihanit – **FBDX**
(438) Eseklet-nisar – **TLPC**

02 *Self-contained energy production*

(98) Setplanis – **LSTP**
(14) Setlvra – **LBD**
(402) Helsata – **0QZ**
(319) Ritva-balanuk – **396**
(22) Litklevu – **R32**

03 *Fully-used, complete pranic circuit*

(3) Kasava – **SP1KL**
(21) Irksaba – **9PQ**
(107) Kersanu – **MN8**
(68) Sterabit – **XPL2**
(409) Rutvrabi – **11-2B**

04 *Masterful directiveness within complete surrender*

(13) Elishur – **R2S**
(106) Suhitar – **HIK**
(92) Araksut – **186PT**
(306) Sunuvish-baver – **KP2**
(83) Menetra – **32K**

05 *Withdrawing from the games of mirrors*

(168) Erektu – **V3P**
(32) Esteva – **TL4**
(418) Kirivirspata – **11-18**
(61) Iranut – **92-LP**
(16) Erseta – **ST11**

06 *Existence beyond body, soul and spirit*

(298) Harasatvi-balush – **926**
(86) Bitrenek – **FRTV**
(113) Narekva – **2P9L**
(28) Kusana – **SL6**
(440) Nukbara – **VKL**

07 *Timelessness through surrender*

(99) Risita – **RWXP**
(111) Brihanu – **32LV**
(34) Ikbarut – **3BQ**
(6) Ritsahur – **KPL2**
(108) Mektaru – **L2T**

08 *Fluid release of linear time*

(44) Mileves – **04P**
(308) Eleshner – **VR2**
(92) Araksut – **186PT**
(11) Nenesa – **S19H**
(86) Bitrenek – **FRTV**

09 *Spacelessness through appreciative perspectives*

(16) Erseta – **ST11**
(410) Hanasat – **4TS**
(116) Ninerek – **3H5L**
(324) Suhach-ornit – **VSP**
(19) Iresta – **SQL**

10 *Existing as the impervious source of our reality*

(110) Vilestu – **MP9**
(62) Subarut – **3R6**
(402) Helsata – **0QZ**
(317) Serchsavir – **QRS**
(86) Bitrenek – **FRTV**

11 *Innovative dancer of the eternal song*

(116) Ninerek – **3H5L**
(264) Asabak-akrich – **KS99**
(98) Setplanis – **LSTP**
(211) Hurusut – **LST8**
(4) Ritubi – **N26-11**

12 *Allowing the joyous shaping of our ever-renewing form*

(89) Lineret – **XKUT**
(164) Kavanit – **95Q**
(32) Esteva – **TL4**
(116) Ninerek – **3H5L**
(72) Isanus – **XL28**

13 *Delightful miracle of expression as form*

(160) Resavit – **SB2**
(432) Nasaru – **3SX**
(86) Bitrenek – **FRTV**
(114) Kirsena – **XYST**
(3) Kasava – **SP1KL**

14 *Inspired enthusiasm of self-regenerating form*

(12) Rusana – **KS2L**
(326) Biraset – **32S**
(81) Setpliher – **VP9**
(92) Araksut – **186PT**
(6) Ritsahur – **KPL2**

15 *Victorious expression of incorruptible matter*

(184) Gravanik – **14P**
(28) Kusana – **SL6**
(69) Rasanur – **46BD**
(421) Herenit – **KPS**
(18) Pruhanas – **MO6**

16   *Strengthened conviction of miraculous existence*

(62) Subarut – **3R6**

(31) Lukvanot – **R2S**

(16) Erseta – **ST11**

(214) Rutpahur – **6T-S11**

(408) Hesta-misech – **HZV**

17   *Marveling at the awakened gifts of the body*

(119) Retsavi – **19ST**

(23) Ristave – **KS2**

(84) Ururuk – **49ST**

(316) Meshpahur-akrat – **PA2**

(298) Harasatvi-balush – **926**

18   *Interpretive dancer of the joyous dance of Infinite expression*

(80) Rinahur – **L2T3**

(61) Iranut – **92-LP**

(312) Gelshanadoch – **LPT**

(98) Setplanis – **LSTP**

(16) Erseta – **ST11**

19   *The gentle guidance of the subtle currents of the ocean of Infinite existence*

(140) Arakva – **2BD**

(116) Ninerek – **3H5L**

(380) Nereksu – **VRX**

(6) Ritsahur – **KPL2**

(91) Arsata – **HRK4**

20   *Childlike wonderment and glad expectations*

(14) Setlvra – **LBD**

(83) Menetra – **32K**

(46) Setkranat – **94PT**

(418) Kirivirspata – **11-18**

(321) Prekpranuhish – **ST3**

21 *Open receptivity to the unfathomable wonders of existence*

(110) Vilestu – **MP9**
(210) Nenklitparu – **32SF**
(93) Pisiter – **LT45**
(2) Mistaba – **NX4-6**
(11) Nenesa – **S19H**

22 *The adventure of never-ending, aware self-discovery*

(16) Erseta – **ST11**
(46) Setkranat – **94PT**
(391) Kiranat – **LPHV**
(429) Barastu – **R20**
(112) Silvatu – **KRS**

23 *Freedom from limiting expectations by readiness to be amazed*

(16) Erseta – **ST11**
(92) Araksut – **186PT**
(247) Harsat-manuvech – **41ST**
(122) Asavit – **KV13**
(84) Ururuk – **49ST**

24 *Self-generated inspiration for the graceful artistry of expression*

(62) Subarut – **3R6**
(81) Setpliher – **VP9**
(329) Sutrivat – **PL2**
(168) Erektu – **V3P**
(26) Skarut – **2SK**

25 *Cooperation of individuality within inclusiveness*

(81) Setpliher – **VP9**
(416) Ukreta – **SK16**
(291) Platplasur – **XPL2**
(362) Karatu – **LV5**
(17) Niretu – **04T**

26 *Living with deliberate reverence through awareness*

(114) Kirsena – **XYST**
(83) Menetra – **32K**
(42) Harchtu – **P3L**
(61) Iranut – **92-LP**
(320) Niskaret – **QP11**

27 *Archetypal awareness of the potency of choices*

(16) Erseta – **ST11**
(43) Setar – **9WK**
(389) Ranuret – **SL16**
(118) Esetur – **LK14**
(26) Skarut – **2SK**

28 *Effortless movement through eternity*

(84) Ururuk – **49ST**
(42) Harchtu – **P3L**
(169) Melkor – **LBX**
(32) Esteva – **TL4**
(319) Ritva-balanuk – **396**

29 *Being our own source of boundless vitality*

(169) Melkor – **LBX**
(32) Esteva – **TL4**
(419) Nensarahik – **VSRT**
(22) Litklevu – **R32**
(318) Kirsh-pater – **L8P**

30 *Effortless miraculous achievements without end*

(72) Isanus – **XL28**
(183) Nanasit – **SL9**
(416) Ukreta – **SK16**
(86) Bitrenek – **FRTV**
(391) Kiranat – **LPHV**

HOW TO DO THE CEREMONY

- Make a stack of the 30 sigils of the Principles of Perpetual Self-Regeneration. Number 1 will be on the top, number 30 on the bottom.

- Place the Rose Template of Codes below the 30 sigils.

- Place the DNA Rose below the rose template of codes†.

- Place the Wheel for Timeless Perpetual Regeneration below the DNA Rose.

- Align the stars and clip the stack together to prevent displacement. Place the stack below your feet as you lie down on your back.

- Place the stack of the 441 angel names beneath your back (behind the navel).

- Have the list of 30 Principles of Perpetual Self-Regeneration in your hand, with their codes and angels.

- Read them one by one, with their 5 angels and the 5 codes, as you feel each one's sigil move up through your feet and all the way up through the top of your head.

- When you have envisioned all 30 sigils moving through you, then envision first the Rose Code Template, and then the DNA Rose, followed by the Wheel for Timeless Per-petual Regeneration, move through you from the feet all the way through.

End by saying:

May the necessary DNA chambers be activated to bring about the Perpetual Self-Regeneration of the incorruptible matter of my body. May the angel gods support this by activating the corresponding cosmic components.

---

† The DNA Rose represents a cross-section, not only of an advanced god being's DNA, showing the frequency cham-bers as petals, but also as a cosmic template. The cosmos has the same pattern of 'sound chambers' as the DNA strand.

Magic Through Emphases: The Magic of the Gods

THIRTY MAGICAL ACTIVATION TEMPLATES
FOR CELLULAR REGENERATION

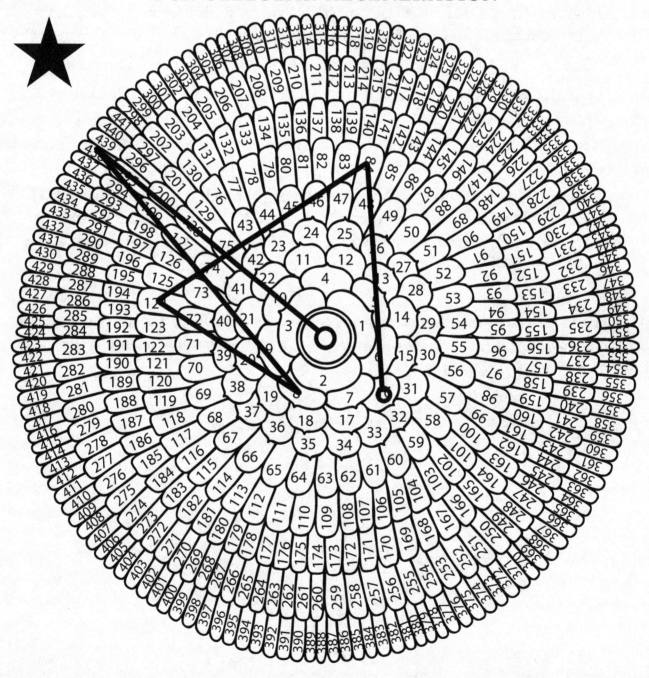

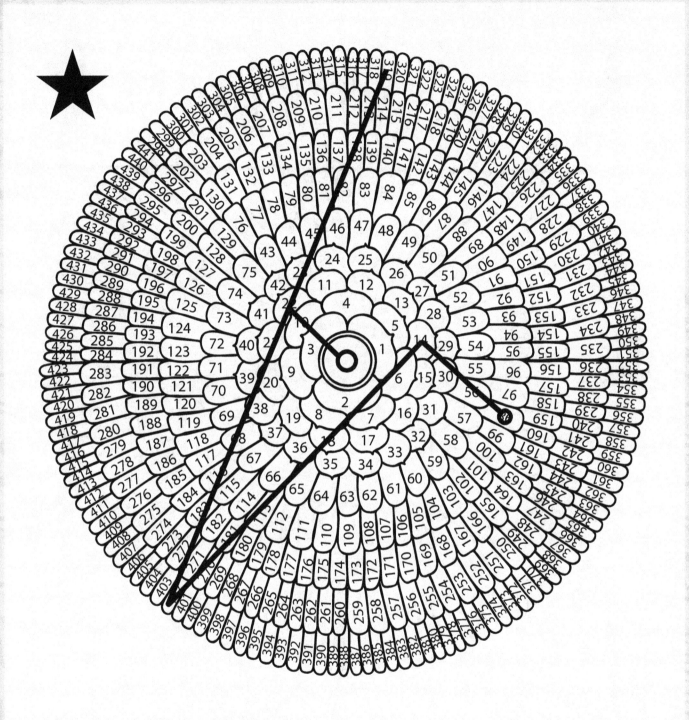

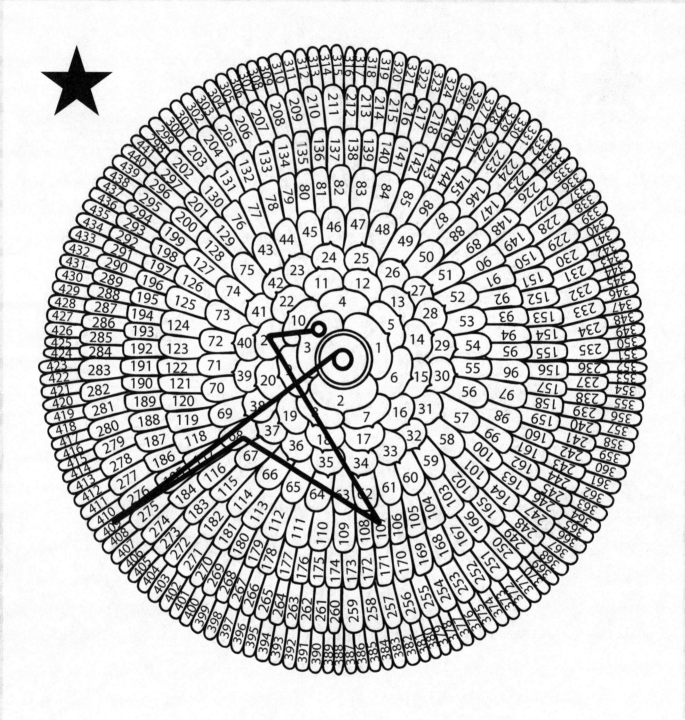

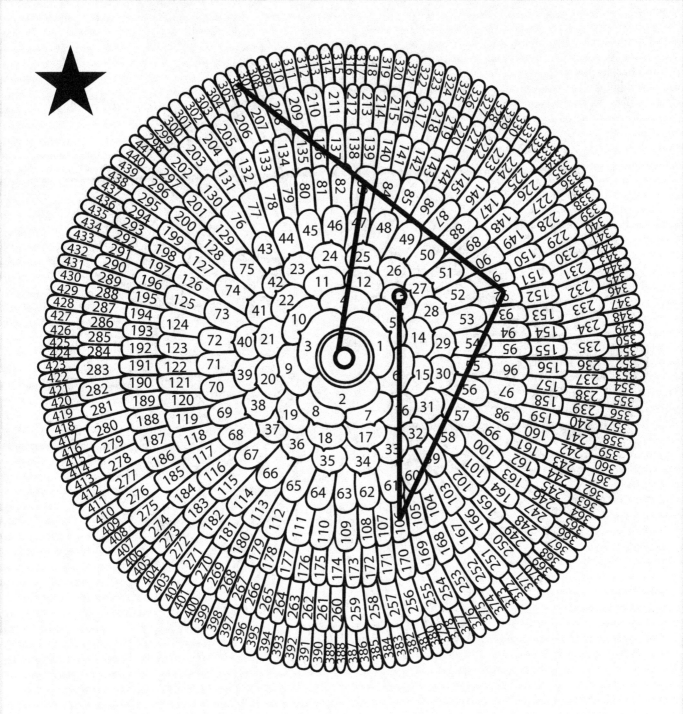

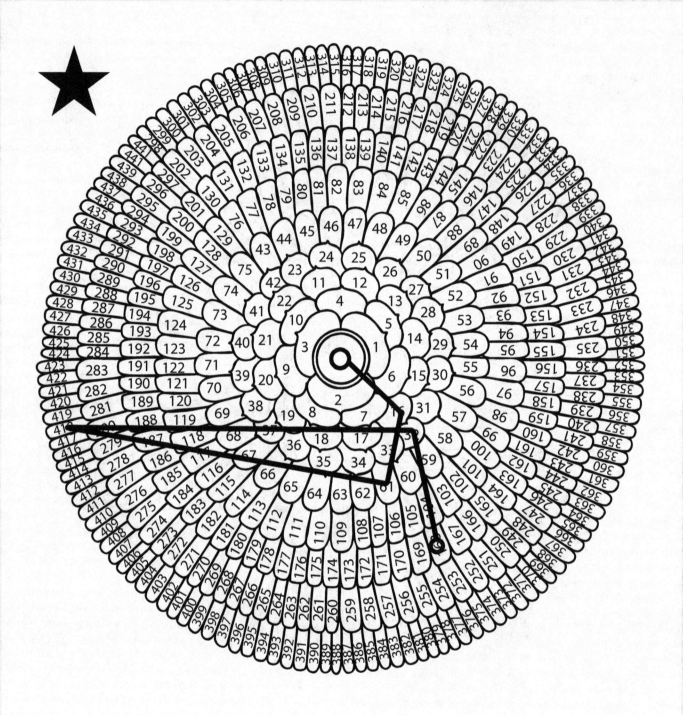

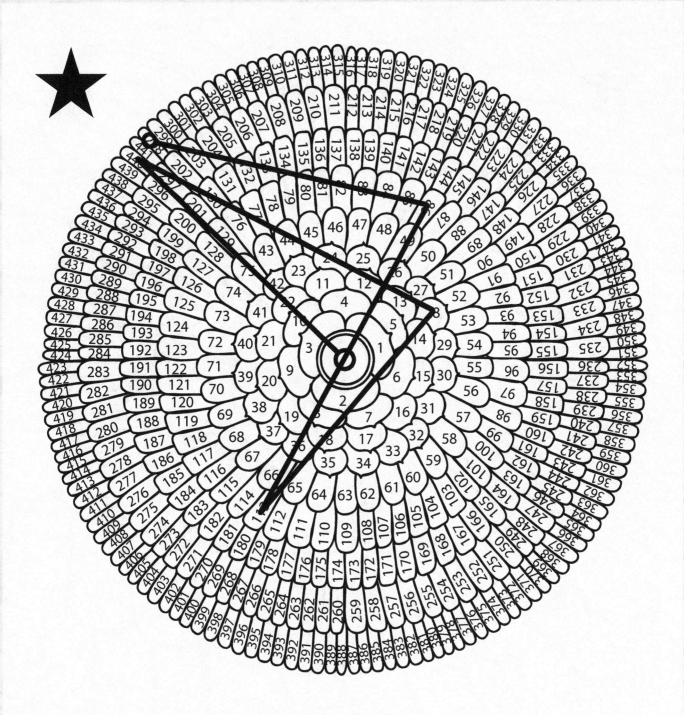

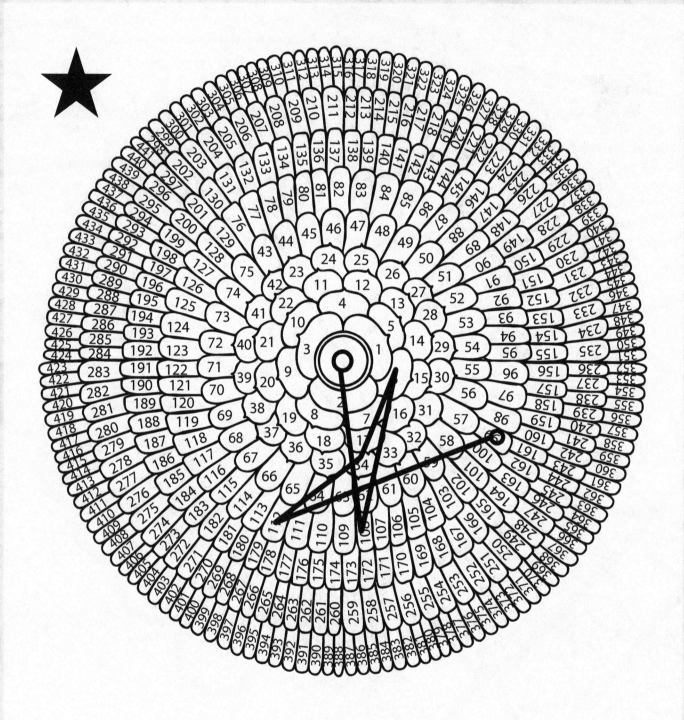

118

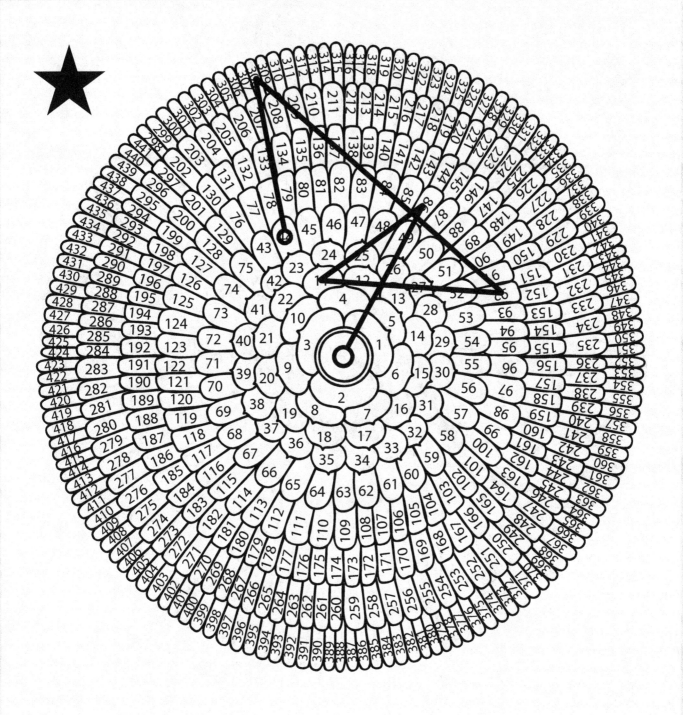

119

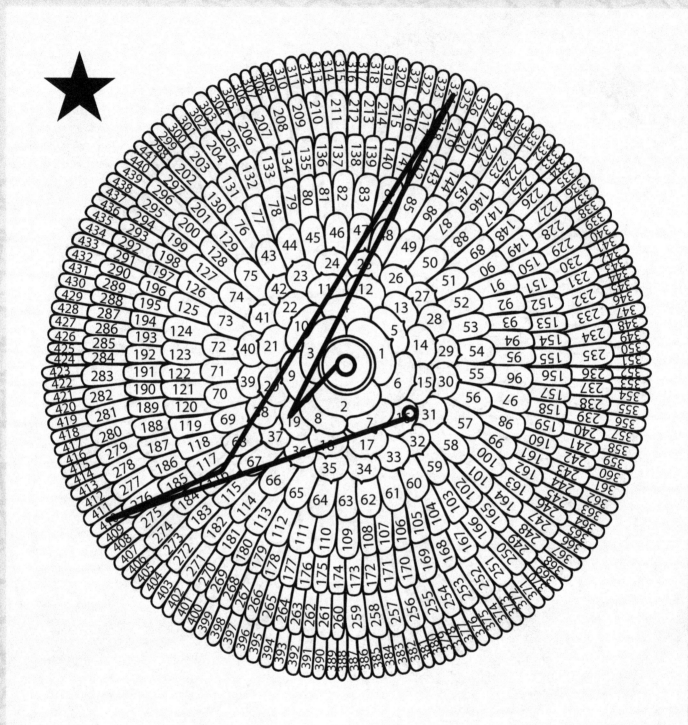

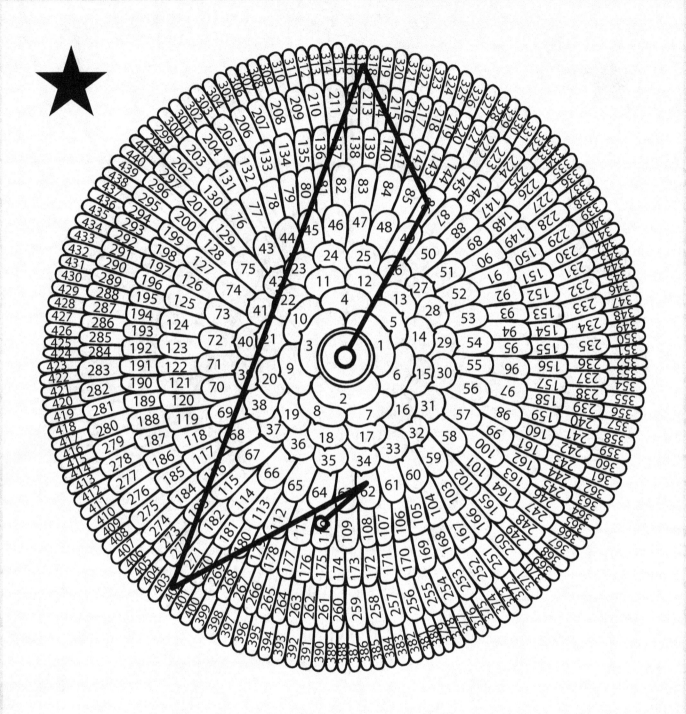

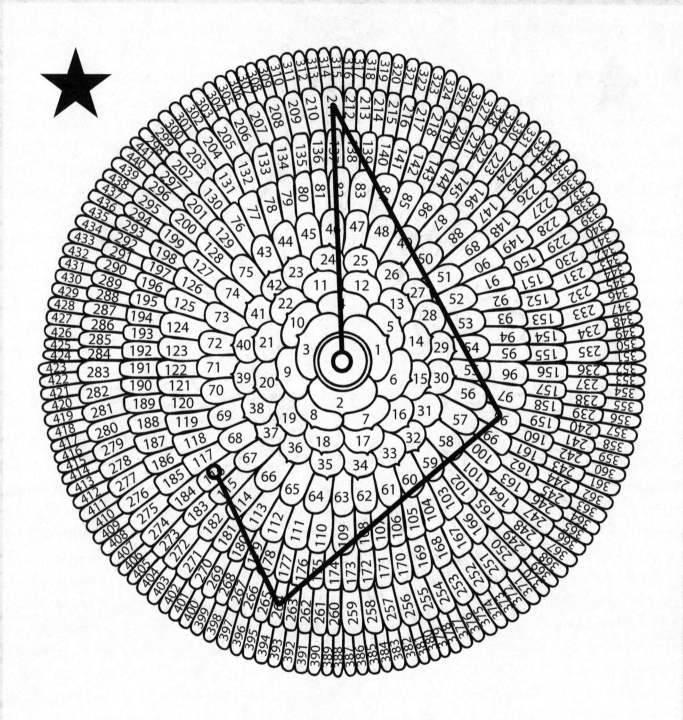

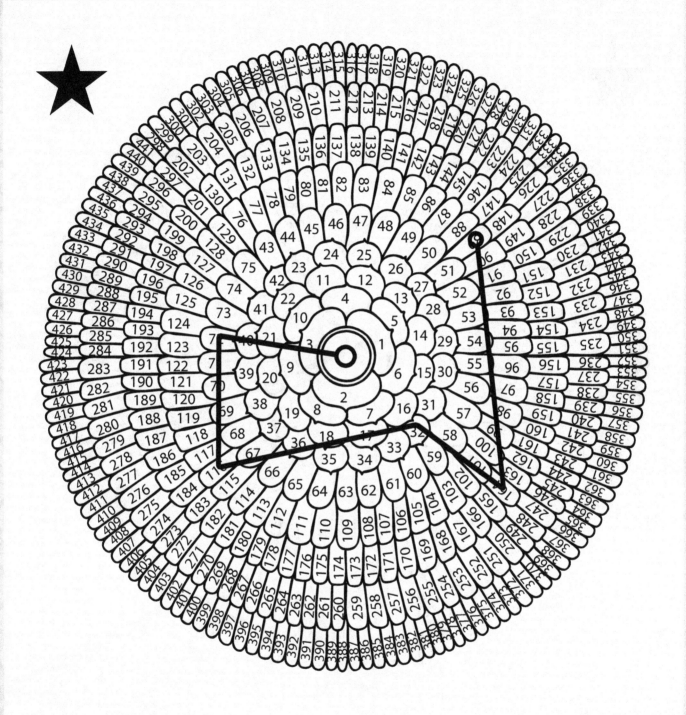

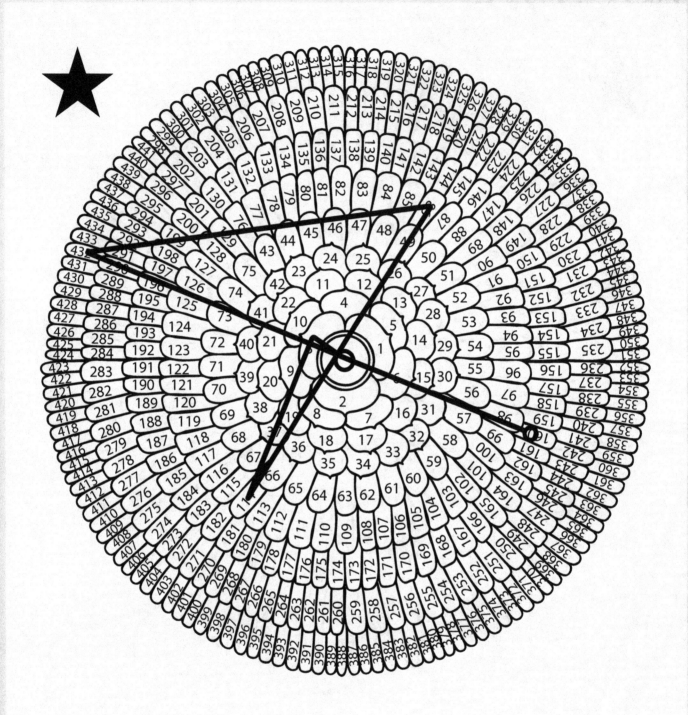

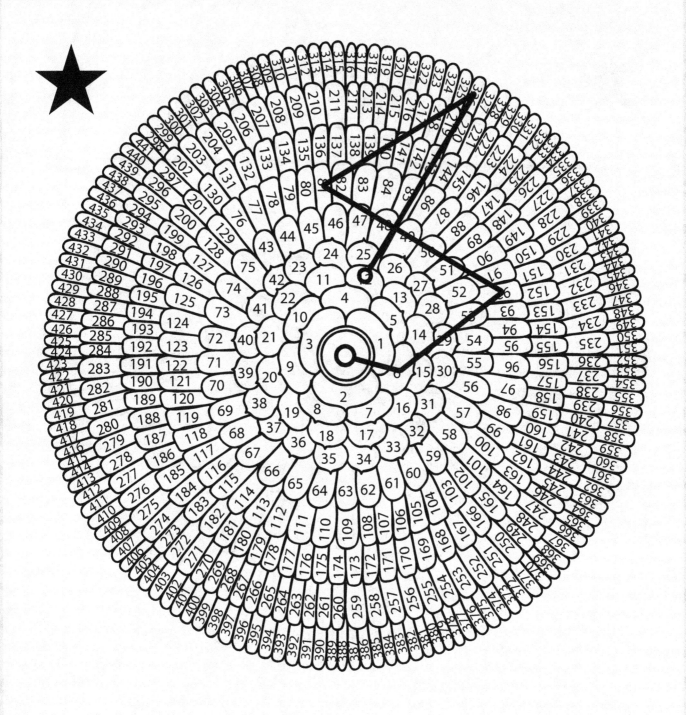

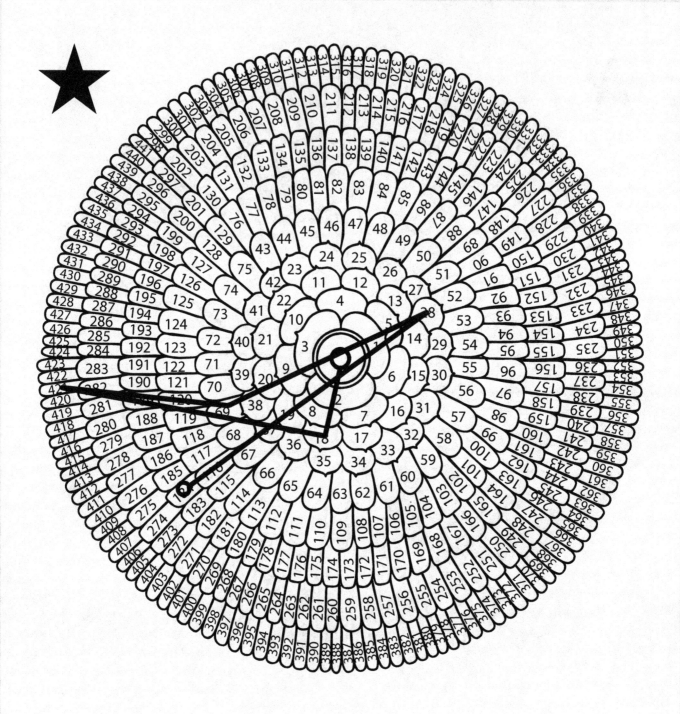

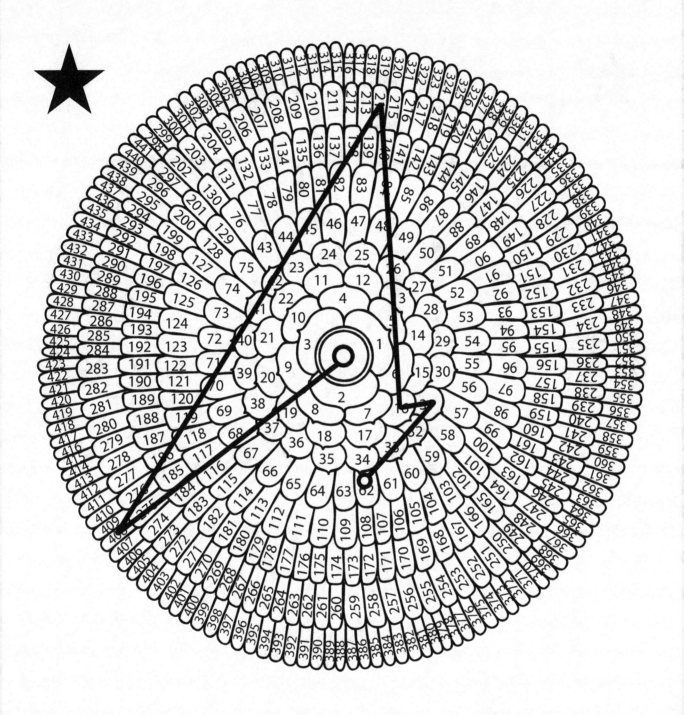

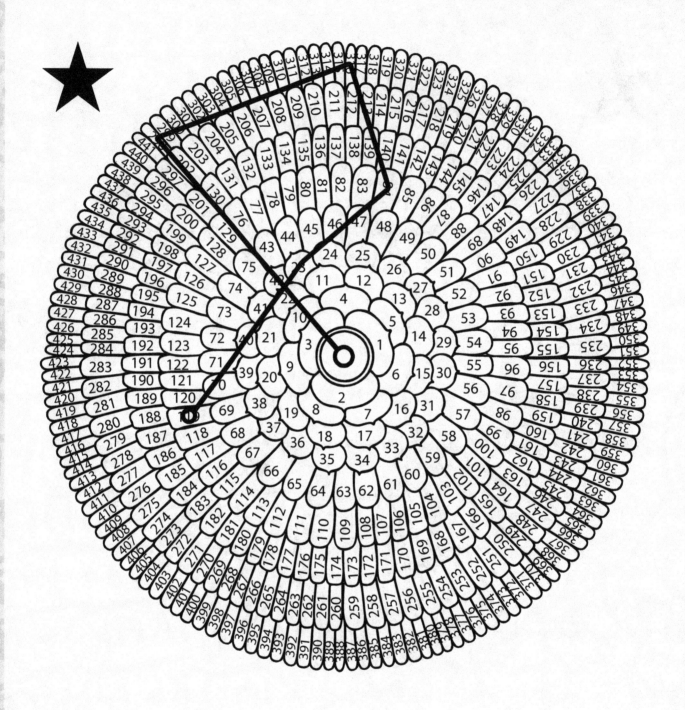

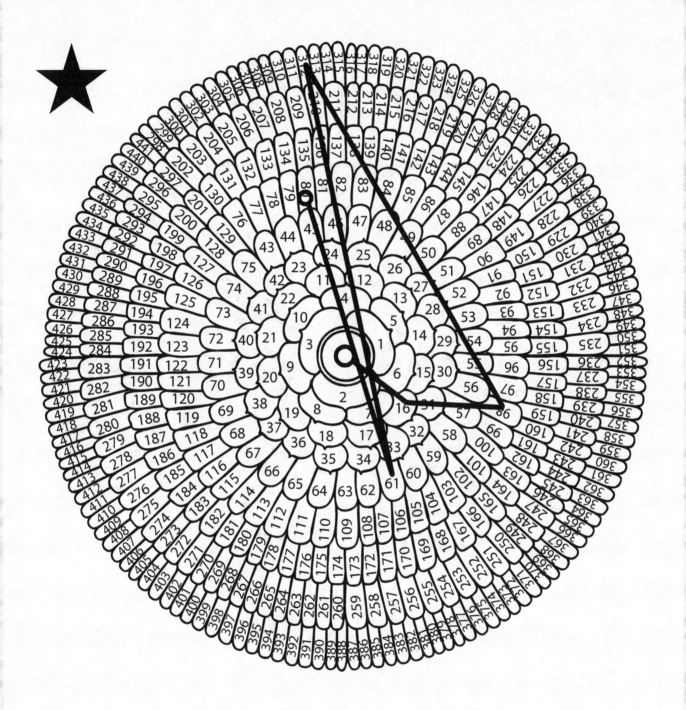

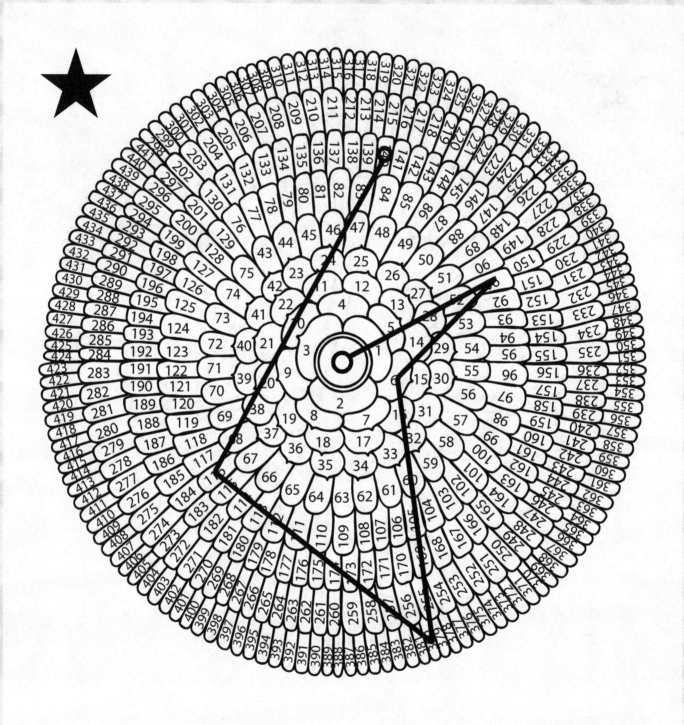

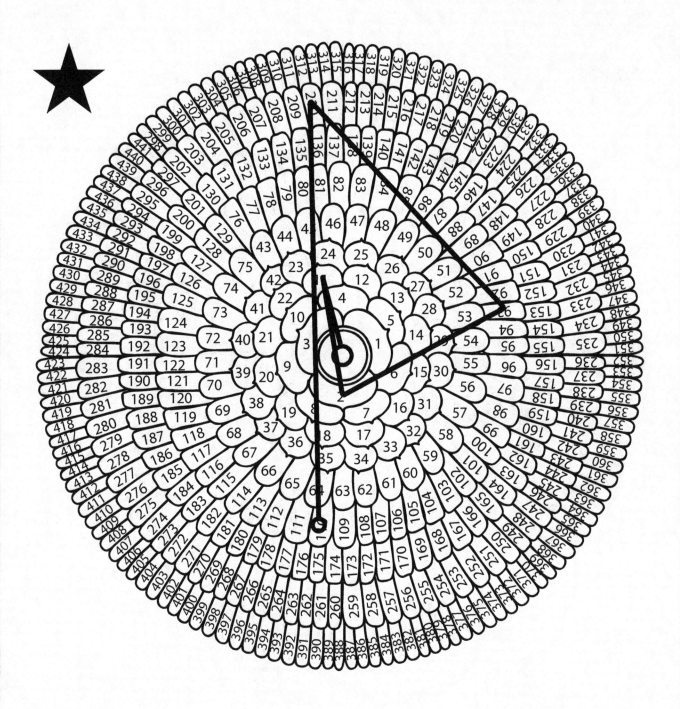

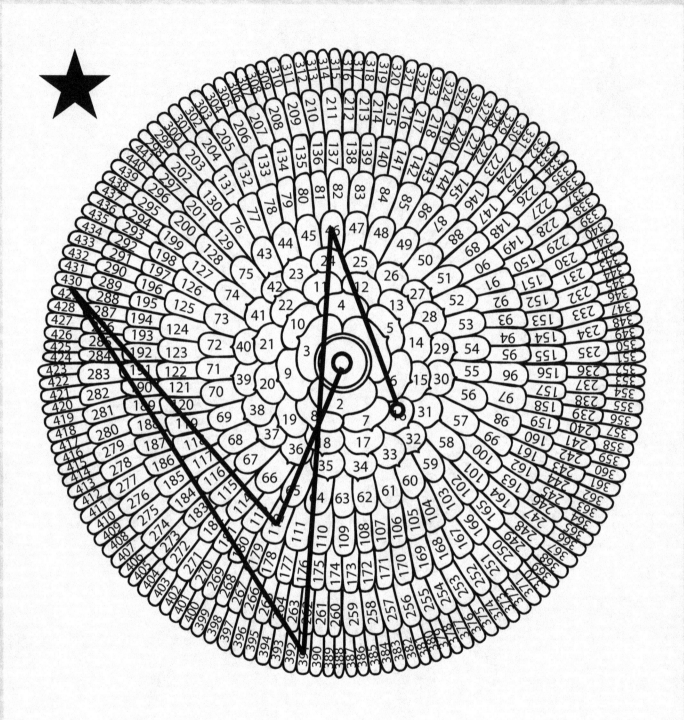

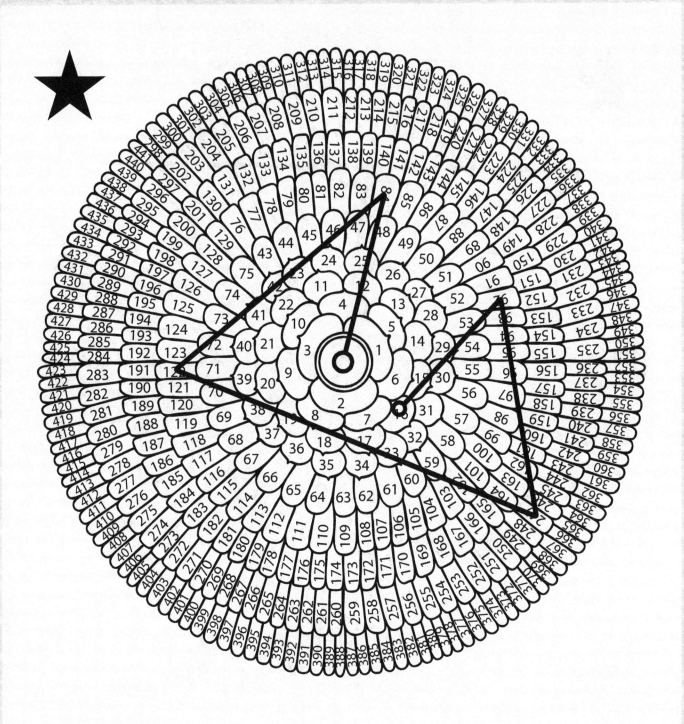

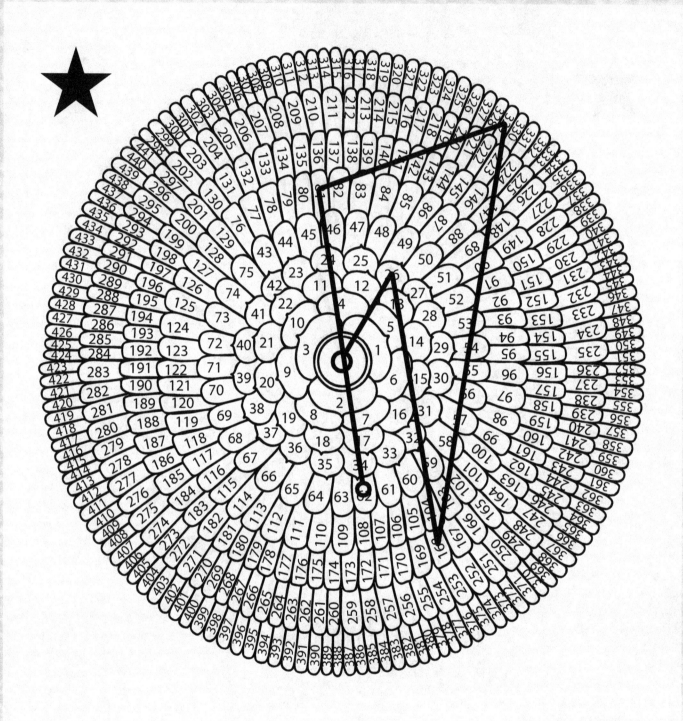

134

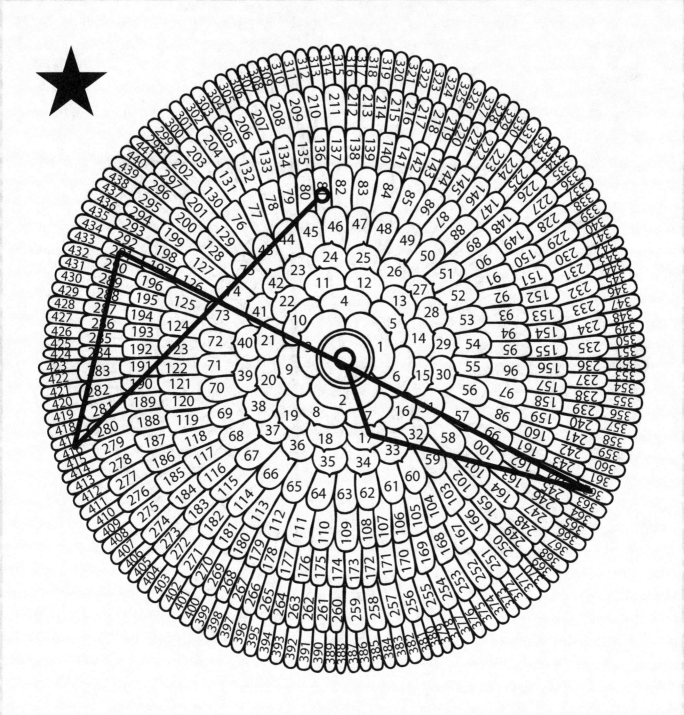

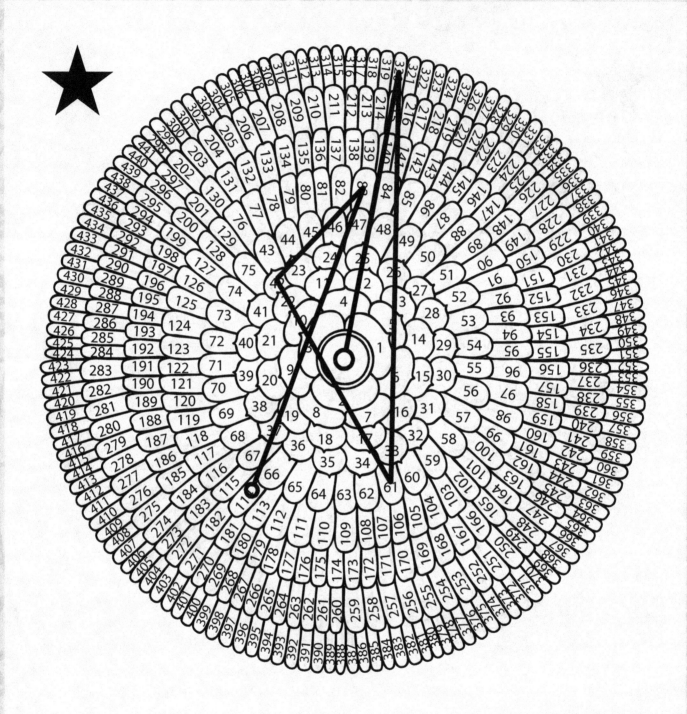

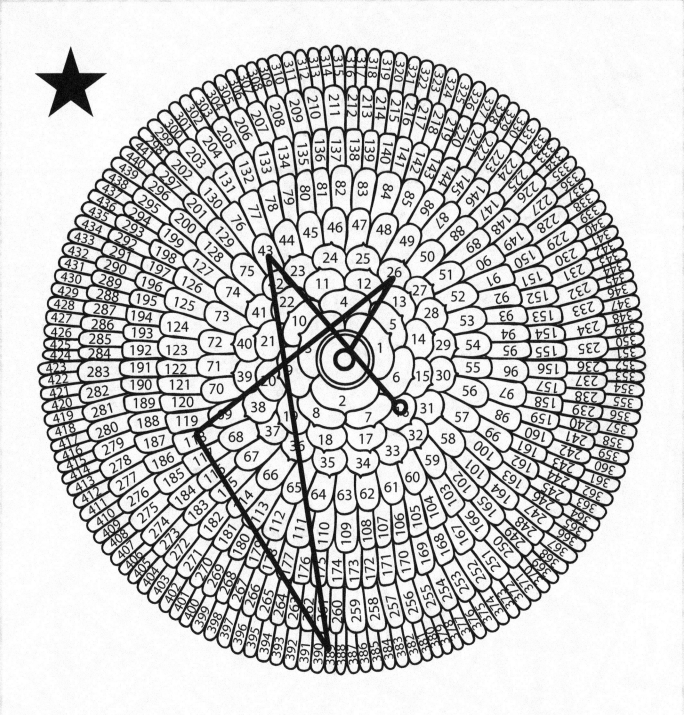

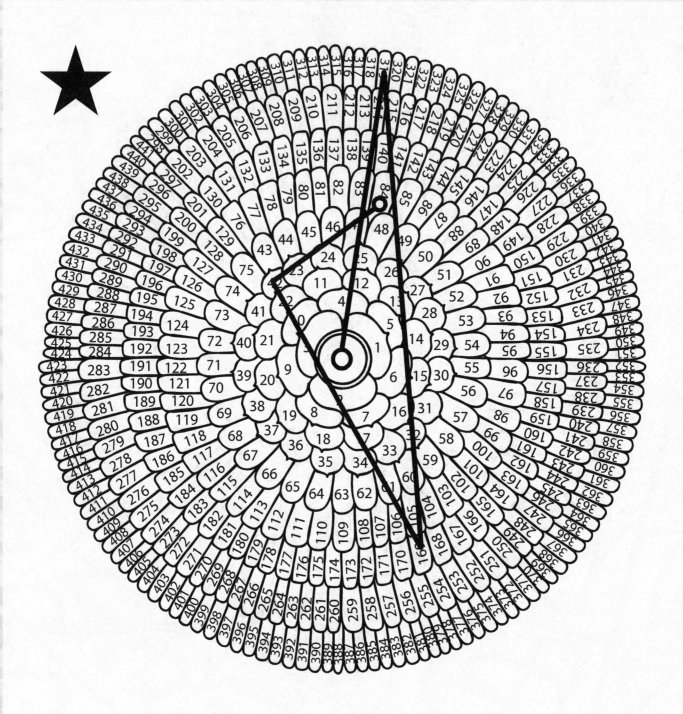

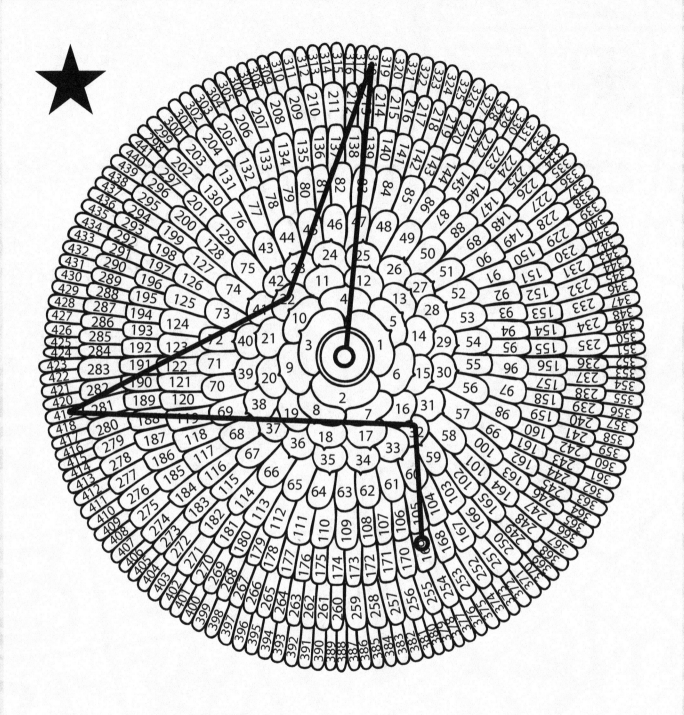

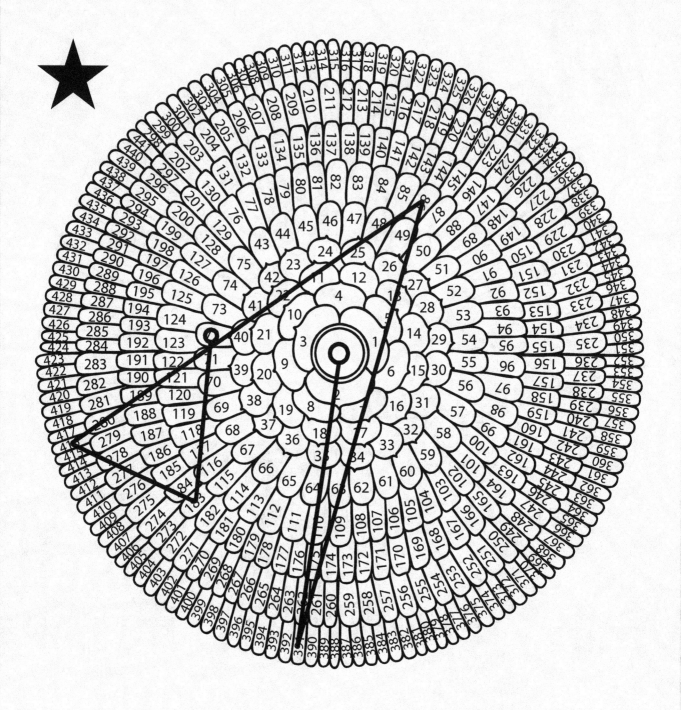

THE DNA ROSE TEMPLATE

THE DNA ROSE TEMPLATE WITH NUMBERS

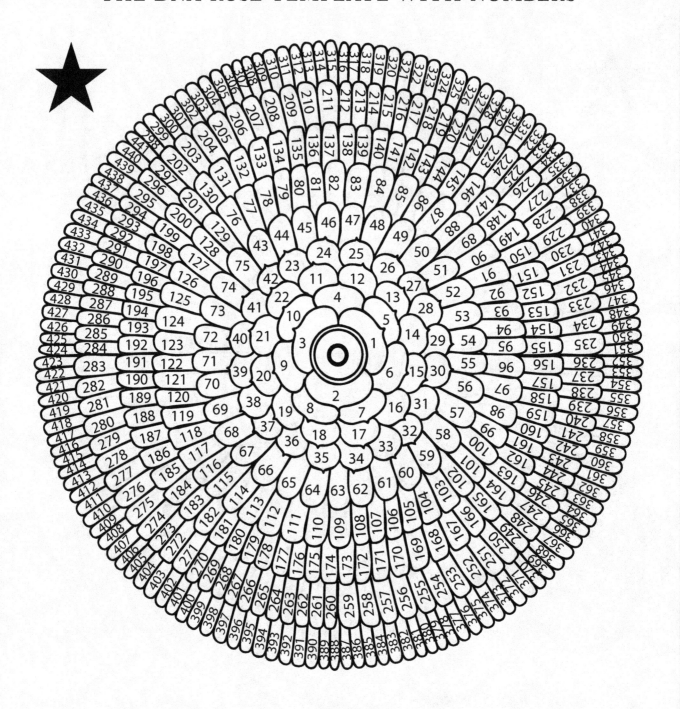

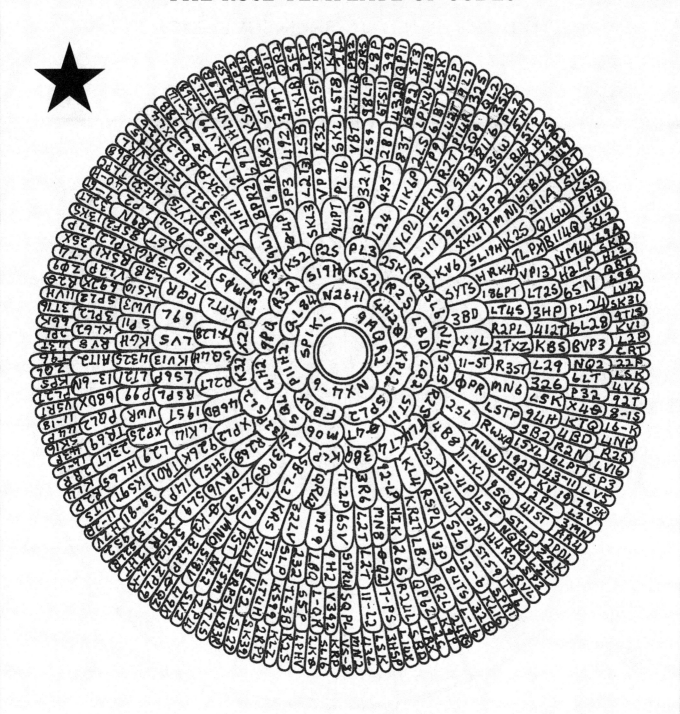

THE WHEEL OF PERPETUAL REGENERATION
THROUGH TRUST IN SELF-SOVEREIGNTY

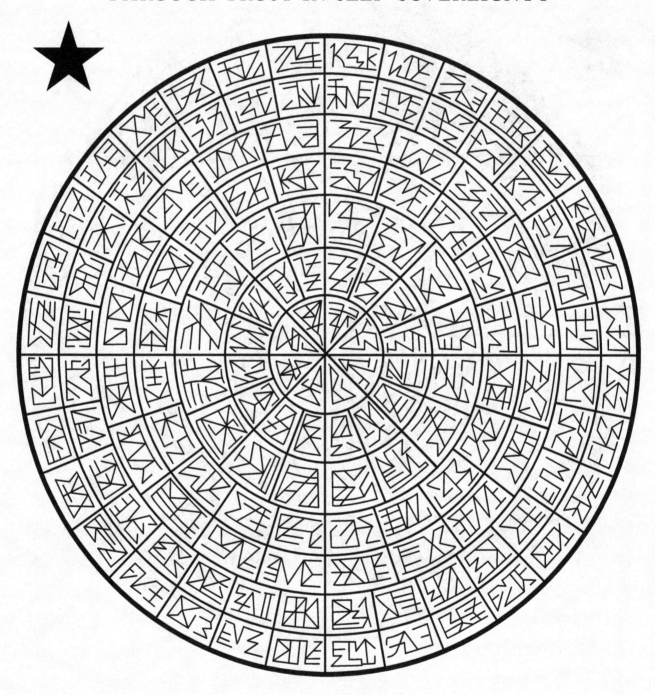

441 ANGEL GODS

01. Saavech	37. Ekselva	73. Misahur
02. Mistaba	38. Kusaru	74. Kurunis
03. Kasava	39. Nesbasur	75. Elsador
04. Ritubi	40. Kiranur	76. Nurata
05. Klisva	41. Utraver	77. Pirahur
06. Ritsahur	42. Harchtu	78. Eskevre
07. Elsena	43. Setar	79. Plehitar
08. Prihanit	44. Mileves	80. Rinahur
09. Kirtlva	45. Hirklana	81. Setpliher
10. Rekpa	46. Setkranat	82. Esklesir
11. Nenesa	47. Usbranot	83. Menetra
12. Rusana	48. Nekbarot	84. Ururuk
13. Elishur	49. Elsavur	85. Seklevra
14. Setlvra	50. Sitklar	86. Bitrenek
15. Sitklavis	51. Viresat	87. Reksavi
16. Erseta	52. Kuraset	88. Ekbaratuk
17. Niretu	53. Erkplasur	89. Lineret
18. Pruhanas	54. Siterek	90. Pelehur
19. Iresta	55. Ilsavit	91. Arsata
20. Kruvrabi	56. Menevech	92. Araksut
21. Irksaba	57. Harsurat	93. Pisiter
22. Litklevu	58. Ikbarnot	94. Karsana
23. Ristave	59. Krusavek	95. Ekranur
24. Arunas	60. Tribarut	96. Hurutat
25. Elerus	61. Iranut	97. Sakravi
26. Skarut	62. Subarut	98. Setplanis
27. Ertreve	63. Ekparahut	99. Risita
28. Kusana	64. Viseklech	100. Arakna
29. Pelevri	65. Barvanuk	101. Mechba-surat
30. Eksavi	66. Lisetar	102. Hersetu
31. Lukvanot	67. Muniter	103. Lakshmet
32. Esteva	68. Sterabit	104. Rutvaba
33. Rasanut	69. Rasanur	105. Nechtaru
34. Ikbarut	70. Kripahar	106. Suhitar
35. Liseter	71. Arasuter	107. Kersanu
36. Nensarat	72. Isanus	108. Mektaru

109. Retvavik	147. Ranavik	185. Krisiter
110. Vilestu	148. Ukrutvravit	186. Karanut
111. Brihanu	149. Helvanit	187. Sihut-ater
112. Silvatu	150. Esklavar	188. Arunasva
113. Narekva	151. Suvanit	189. Viresat
114. Kirsena	152. Hekvravit	190. Runaset
115. Retsahur	153. Karusta	191. Hireklat
116. Ninerek	154. Hespi	192. Marchvador
117. Kilshebas	155. Ranastu	193. Nensurat
118. Esetur	156. Eksahur	194. Rakvaplet
119. Retsavi	157. Mansarat	195. Elsavir
120. Menenus	158. Esatur	196. Hiresta
121. Rasanur	159. Kurinar	197. Arkplahur
122. Asavit	160. Resavit	198. Kerusater
123. Eklet-brabit	161. Elektar	199. Vibrit-klavit
124. Hesetu	162. Mensarut	200. Rasbahut
125. Misarut	163. Ravanik	201. Kalshavit
126. Arsahur	164. Kavanit	202. Brispahur
127. Mesenech	165. Elsaruk	203. Krunavach
128. Elvavis	166. Menserat	204. Hirspahur
129. Kisarut	167. Arukstar	205. Mesbasur
130. Helsatur	168. Erektu	206. Kiletrach
131. Mananes	169. Melkor	207. Esenut
132. Arsahur	170. Rasatu	208. Rasatu
133. Eksuravit	171. Arakvar	209. Hurpahet
134. Menet-klarit	172. Hirskavi	210. Nenklitparu
135. Asur	173. Blivabik	211. Hurusut
136. Herchsaba	174. Urusta	212. Esekra
137. Meserut	175. Harakva	213. Visabach
138. Nanitva	176. Kuhanit	214. Rutpahur
139. Eruk-sartu	177. Lisater	215. Eleru
140. Arakva	178. Gravanuk	216. Harastu
141. Biratet	179. Ritklaver	217. Nesbarut
142. Nensklar	180. Urabik	218. Akravit
143. Urutar	181. Kelsatur	219. Heseklut
144. Virsava	182. Meretur	220. Birespa
145. Akbarut	183. Nanasit	221. Mistubar
146. Melsatur	184. Gravanik	222. Rachmar

223. Blihaspat	261. Pliset-vravi	299. Erebikplatur
224. Kirshbahur	262. Trihasanar	300. Hertl-hasbavi
225. Renesuk	263. Erlalus-vravi	301. Sukret-sabavit
226. Elsklabit	264. Asabak-akrich	302. Rananek
227. Isbaruk	265. Kursunas	303. Palasha
228. Nensahur	266. Siharanus	304. Nensarabruk
229. Kirunat	267. Luvech-vranur	305. Ertl-brasbatur
230. Esebit	268. Selhanus-abi	306. Sunuvish-baver
231. Suchbaver	269. Shrechnanusat	307. Istrach-manut
232. Lihursat	270. Ornasat-huster	308. Eleshner
233. Mirenech	271. Prihanar-salanus	309. Suhuvirtlbi
234. Ursbanit	272. Sersanoch	310. Eksabilanash
235. Reksavur	273. Klibich-aster	311. Brabech-huresvi
236. Orsenat	274. Virserat-usunukvi	312. Gelshanadoch
237. Vribavechvi	275. Gravanech	313. Ursech-partpavi
238. Stahunachvi	276. Kelsutar	314. Karanash-selhatut
239. Splenunitva	277. Hersachvi	315. Vilesmanunit
240. Krinasavur	278. Manunechvi	316. Meshpahur-akrat
241. Urek	279. Blishet-aranas	317. Serchsavir
242. Misavech	280. Kistrar	318. Kirshpater
243. Selhasunet	281. Sihuster	319. Ritva-balanuk
244. Subarut	282. Pripravit-pretesar	320. Niskaret
245. Elsavrik	283. Irinis-vaver	321. Prekpranuhish
246. Interuch	284. Kalanasvi	322. Skertlhat
247. Harsat-manuvech	285. Itruch-balshet	323. Rinesat
248. Tresibaru	286. Avrabit-suter	324. Suhach-ornit
249. Telenot	287. Arkmananes	325. Entre-blavanish
250. Karstu	288. Kirtlva	326. Biraset
251. Hereksa	289. Hurunis	327. Kihur
252. Senechvi	290. Mistral	328. Elsenar
253. Vrevasbaru	291. Platplasur	329. Sutrivat
254. Arneksatu	292. Erskranit	330. Eskrahu
255. Liseret	293. Urukpater	331. Susi-anar
256. Arsanoch	294. Kelkanish	332. Kerstanur
257. Vrisvrabi	295. Gravavit	333. Hilspabit
258. Estavik	296. Erkstabit	334. Truhaspava
259. Sinech-arstu	297. Sechnunanit	335. Kiru-sesavit
260. Sahur-manit	298. Harasatvi-balush	336. Itrihat-ekla

337. Huravit	375. Reneksu	413. Blubech
338. Kilichvar	376. Erektu	414. Suveta
339. Nesusklavet	377. Vrasaru	415. Asba
340. Pitrubar	378. Irikta	416. Ukreta
341. Isterenot	379. Biraret	417. Vruvabik
342. Utribaret	380. Nereksu	418. Kirivirspata
343. Karsahit	381. Balestu	419. Nensarahik
344. Erulestranet	382. Harakta	420. Utrebik
345. Menhuvravit	383. Usava	421. Herenit
346. Asvach-paret	384. Neruk	422. Haraspa
347. Kanahis	385. Avara	423. Mistahur
348. Etrehus	386. Nurparet	424. Blubek
349. Misaravet	387. Haranach	425. Setrevi
350. Kitrubaret	388. Rustahet	426. Nusarut
351. Ananaklavi	389. Ranuret	427. Karanas
352. Utrubaret	390. Vruchtaret	428. Kuvrenot
353. Hespa-kinuves	391. Kiranat	429. Barastu
354. Suhuch-navet	392. Heresatu	430. Heresa
355. Kenenut	393. Misharu	431. Kachbaru
356. Anasa-usabrit	394. Nansaru	432. Nasaru
357. Klirasut	395. Erkplata	433. Kuhetpata
358. Entemplehur	396. Haravit	434. Neklit-aras
359. Nasahus	397. Rusaver	435. Viset-vabru
360. Kinahir	398. Kurunut	436. Uktarut
361. Netrebit	399. Ratvravir	437. Huskel-varavas
362. Karatu	400. Harsatu	438. Eseklet-nisar
363. Hisba	401. Uruk-nanes	439. Avrarut-pleseta
364. Nanek	402. Helsata	440. Nukbara
365. Tra-uva	403. Vibret-urusvi	441. Rasatu
366. Sisatu	404. Harchnahut	
367. Eksaru	405. Sipre-urut	
368. Klisara	406. Harsta-misech	
369. Hekstu	407. Ukru-varasbi	
370. Karanu	408. Hesta-misech	
371. Hareksa	409. Rutvrabi	
372. Nensara	410. Hanasat	
373. Virasta	411. Ukrevi	
374. Husklava	412. Hirkpata	

THE AWAKENING OF THE 30 PRINCIPLES
OF PERPETUAL SELF-REGENERATION

1. Self-sustaining emotional self-sovereignty
2. Self-contained energy production
3. Fully-used, complete pranic circuit
4. Masterful directiveness within complete surrender
5. Withdrawing from the games of mirrors
6. Existence beyond body, soul and spirit
7. Timelessness through surrender
8. Fluid release of linear time
9. Spacelessness through appreciative perspectives
10. Existing as the impervious source of our reality
11. Innovative dancer of the eternal song
12. Allowing the joyous shaping of our ever-renewing form
13. Delightful miracle of expression as form
14. Inspired enthusiasm of self-regenerating form
15. Victorious expression of incorruptible matter
16. Strengthened conviction of miraculous existence
17. Marveling at the awakened gifts of the body
18. Interpretive dancer of the joyous dance of Infinite expression
19. The gentle guidance of the subtle currents of the ocean of Infinite existence
20. Childlike wonderment and glad expectations
21. Open receptivity to the unfathomable wonders of existence
22. The adventure of never-ending, aware self-discovery
23. Freedom from limiting expectations by readiness to be amazed
24. Self-generated inspiration for the graceful artistry of expression
25. Cooperation of individuality within inclusiveness
26. Living with deliberate reverence through awareness
27. Archetypal awareness of the potency of choices
28. Effortless movement through eternity
29. Being our own source of boundless vitality
30. Effortless miraculous achievements without end

Entering Godhood: The Highest Calling
http://goo.gl/YbCDo

Chant of the Angel Gods: Music for God Magic
http://goo.gl/jy3o3

How to Release Yourself from Previously Binding
Spiritual Contracts
http://goo.gl/gxvvr

Discourse 6
The Commitment to Life

Q. Is there any reason other than belief systems formed from social conditioning, as to why death has such a foothold amongst humanity?

A. The first reason is guilt. The body, soul and spirit struggle for supremacy, and control in our lives. While alive, the body is in control. Spirit tries to tell us that the body is an unholy and unworthy vehicle for our existence. Thus, we try and prove that we are worthy of life…

Q. What about the higher stages of evolution during physical life, which part of us is in control then?

A. It becomes a collaboration: integrated diversity. In a resurrected being, body, soul and spirit combine to form a vehicle of expression consisting of spiritualized, or incorruptible, matter.

Q. Are there other reasons why death persists?

A. Most are not fully committed to life, and we have a sentimental view of death as a place of blissful repose, constructed to comfort those who lose loved ones.

Q. Why aren't we committed to life, excluding the possibility that we don't feel worthy of it?

A. The further that we've evolved, the less we feel at home, and the less we are able to embrace worldly things. When a major perception-changing event takes place, it can produce a perceptual crises: Nothing seems to make sense, what matters to others no longer matters to us, and it is possible to lose touch with loved ones. These are times when ones commitment to life can become very shaky – not what one would expect from a spiritually developed life. It just seems that the rest of the world is mad, that their pursuits are shallow, and that their aggression and other baser instincts pollute ones space.

Q. How can one prevent that? It's everywhere!

A. By finding a little corner of this world, like your home or room, that is your inner sanctum, your holy space. Realize that it is the stage of your evolved reality. Each lives in their own reality, and the insane reality of others, is not your reality. You can reject things of the world that seep into your reality. Say firmly: "I dissolve this reality... My reality unfolds with grace, ease and elegance," and banish these thoughts, while replacing them with images of things of nature that make you happy. Interact sparingly with those who do not inspire you, and above all, guard the motives behind your actions to make sure they're not done to live up to others' expectations or to pander, or try to please others.

Q. How does one regain the love of life, when we have become disenchanted with it?

A. When one hits such a bleak spot in one's eternal journey, change the way that you look at the folly of man. Don't think of it as life, but as a procession of folly in the pageantry of life, like jesters and harlequins moving in a procession across the stage of life. If one takes the folly of man seriously, it can cause anger, grief, and depression – just stay in the observer mode. On the stage of eternity, this too will pass.

Q. When that empty feeling hits, what else can one do?

A. We are so used to identifying with our worldviews and using our belief systems (our personal matrices) as reference points within the vastness of our being, that the 'empty' feeling can cause anxiety. Just realize that these dramatic transitions are part of our external existence, doing a spring-cleaning. It is time to reinvent how we express our environment, time for dramatic changes. Don't be afraid of the 'emptying out' of what once mattered. This is a chance to dream in a new existence.

Q. What else can precipitate this reality crisis in how we relate to the world?

A. For me, it has also occurred when something has shocked my innocence – such as the maliciousness I encounter in seeing a demon. It seems that living in a world where there is such malevolence is not acceptable. It has taken some soul searching for me to reconcile it through the following realizations: There is no part of reality that I can encounter that isn't an expression of an aspect of myself. Instead of denying something the right to exist, I find what part of me that it represents, evolve it through perception, and in doing so, all life evolves as well.

Q. Where did you find such malevolence within you, if I may ask?

A. In the cruel way in which I've treated myself. I would, for instance, not dream of having someone else work at the grueling pace that I have set for myself, whereas for years, I had no wages at all. That's enslavement. The lack of acceptance that people give their own bodies, always trying to fix something, is extremely non-enhancing.

Q. How does one dream in a new reality?

A. One can't be too rigid about how life should be. The transformational release of the old will have opened up undreamed of opportunities by releasing previously unobtainable energy. Because the future is as yet unknown, think of it as a labyrinth. The key is to take a rest if the experience has been very traumatic, and then when you're ready to, start moving. Follow every passage of opportunity, and if it doesn't lead anywhere, turn around and follow another. But keep exploring.

Q. When you're in a slump like that, where do you begin?

A. In mythology, there is a golden thread that leads you to the heart of the labyrinth. Find the end of the thread and follow it through the labyrinth. Find the one thing that stirs a current of inspiration, no matter how faint the stirring is, and pursue it. The golden thread is the thread of inspiration.

Q. And if nothing stirs you?

A. Then rest in passivity a while longer until life starts to beckon.

Q. What does one do when death beckons, when you're in a position of crises – where one has to decide between life and death?

A. Firstly, remind yourself that the death that's beckoning is the dying to the old way of being, not the death of your body. You are a timeless, incorruptible being and to surrender your power to the illusion of death is unworthy of an incorruptible master's life. Life is challenging you to create and express a new reality.

The Linear Stages of Change

TRANSFORMATION

As we grow in awareness, and problems are recognized for what they truly are (opportunities for growth), they lose their hold on us and we no longer need them. Suddenly circumstances in our lives seem to change. Friendships fall by the wayside, jobs may become obsolete and we find life flowing a lot more effortlessly as it transforms before our eyes.

This stage is marked by so many changes that it can be called the time of the death of the old. If we hold on longer than we should to relationships or situations, we find life shedding them for us through forced change. This time can certainly be disconcerting, as the old platform we stood on disintegrates, but the energy released when that which no longer serves us drops away, is a great reward. With increased energy comes new experiences, and ease in meeting old challenges that bring a sense of deep self-satisfaction. As one sheds the old, the body responds by purifying itself. Toxins release and the body can hold more light.

TRANSMUTATION

After transformation sheds the unnecessary parts of our lives, the true challenges stand revealed. This phase is the one where most people get stuck. Mindlessly feeling victimized by the very experiences their higher selves designed for them, they fail to turn pain to wisdom, judgment to compassion. The very essence of transmutation is to turn something of a lower frequency into a higher frequency; the alchemical process of turning lead to gold.

During the phase of transmutation, we are confronted with never before encountered challenges or those we have failed to learn from. Life has just served the ball across the net and waits for our response. The harder the serve, the more we can gain. Most people spend their whole life running away from the balls coming across the net instead of hitting them back.

If we can find the lessons and insights of our challenges, we score enough points to move on to the next game. If we are very diligent, we can even gain insights on behalf of others, increasing our points on the scoreboard. The insights we gain during this stage must be tested to turn them into experiential knowledge.

TRANSFIGURATION

Major transfigurations such as disconnecting from ego-identification (becoming God-conscious), and entering into Immortal Mastery come but a few times in one's life. All change, however, follows this exact map with its three stages. The larger transfigurations are just more noticeable. Even the little changes add up, eventually allowing enough light into our lives for our entire life to transfigure. As more and more clarity is gained, the person must transfigure in order to accommodate the increased light.

The joyous truth is that there is no end to progression. When we have made it through all the evolutionary stages of man's awareness, we shall move even beyond that ultimate goal of humanness: Immortal Mastery. Beyond lies the god kingdom where we can come and go with the speed of thought throughout all realms of time and space – the cosmos as our playground.

Q. How is reality formed?

A. It requires 16 pillars to hold up the new stage, or reality, that you will be reinventing your expression on. The 16 pillars are unique for each person. Here is how to create the pillars:

Step 1

Scan the dream that has been your life's past. Identify 16 memories of contented happiness.

Step 2

Analyze what factor made the particular memory satisfying. These are the 16 factors you want to build a new life on.

For example, I remember being about four years old, and travelling in the back seat of my parent's car, dressed in my nighty with little owls on it, to see Tarzan at the drive-in theater. My mother had made little meat pies to eat on our trip. The deep sense of adventure and contentment I felt came from:

1. Our car was a separate and holy space, warmed by a little girl's happiness.

   Factor: create your own individualized spaces, even at the office, in which your noble emotions can express.

2. Elements of self-nurturing made me feel supported even when I was out in the world.

   Factor: Food to eat, a pillow, and my favorite blanket in case I got tired, created a feeling of self-support.

3. The anticipation of safely experiencing Tarzan's adventures.

   Factor: Your being is your sustenance, and you are designing the fulfillment of glad expectations. Trust the benevolence of your own design.

Step 3

Revisit these factors every day of your new life. In times of emptiness, revisiting the feelings that you felt during happy moments is a good idea.

Step 4

You can develop affirmations for daily use around these factors, such as:

- My being is my sustenance.
- I trust my own self-support.
- I love, nurture and accept my physical form.
- I am an incorruptible, timeless master of my own reality.

Q. How long must we repeat the affirmations we design for ourselves?

A. For at least 60 days. When a disempowering thought comes up, say firmly: "I reject that reality," and then repeat your aphorisms. You can also immediately envision at least one thing that you would like to have in your future, and finish by holding that vision and saying, "I express this reality".

Q. You've said that as we evolve, life around us is evolved also. Can we turn demons to angels, for example?

A. Well, they have two completely different functions. Angels embody order, and demons embody the unknown, or chaos. Angels hold the structure of a reality, and demons hold the destructuring. Although demons don't turn into something else, they nevertheless can express at a much higher level as we clear our own inner demons: the areas where we are not expressing our highest vision.

Q. You have said that there are god beings among us, that the god reality is a different reality than that of man, though co-existing in the same space on Earth. Is the god reality formed by pillars, (concepts or illuminations) as well?

A. Yes, 441 concepts embodied by angel gods.

Prophecy of the Gods from the Library of the White Horse

16TH PLATE, PART IV

Kee-eehana birak heras paret harestu

Among us they walk, but we know them not

They hide among the ordinary where none know to seek

Immortal they are and never death shall see

Some through time tunnels came to walk with man,

Others for thousands of years have lived on the land

Some in isolation watch over human affairs

Most reside among men, though none know they're there

They overcome illusions that man might see

This is why they assume infirmities

When these records, holy and pure,

Are once again read, they need no longer endure

Let them from this service be set free

Let the God-Kingdom arise in majesty

Daily Meditations to Access New Potential

1. Spend time in a preparatory meditation going deep into silence, just to get to know the feeling or sight of your box (which is just a useful toy to achieve communication with that which lies outside of life's accessibility). Once you are able to call up your box in meditation, proceed as follows.

2. Imagine the box lid opening as you go into deep meditation. Inside is a projector that projects a scene for you to look at. Write it down.

3. Go back into meditation and wait for a second scene. Write it down. Continue in this way until the images stop. Come out of meditation.

4. Try to recall the feelings and any additional background impressions of the scenes to flesh them out and make them more complete.

5. Try and connect as many of these short scenes into a story or several little pieces of a story. You can make up small connective links.

6. Do this daily and the stories will become more coherent. They may however stay unlike the logic-based, cerebral stories we are used to. If you have not been able to connect the scenes, this is still successful.

    It is not in connecting the dots of the scenes that makes this technique successful, but in the non-cognitive knowingness that floods through (and reaches us at a deep level) between the images. The changes brought about by doing this meditation as a daily practice will become obvious in subtle but profound ways.

Messages from Untapped Potential

1. The cosmos we are in is like a blue dwarf. We are as a cosmos surrounded by an orange sun. When the blue sun expands into the orange sun, we become an enlarged white giant, having the full spectrum of light to express Infinite life.

2. The children shall become the elders in their ability to access unyielded potential through imagery.

3. The blue ball, which is our Cosmos, is a dense sphere that does not allow light through – its surface is a mirror. Life in the surrounding orange 'sun' has contracted into egocentricity because of its obsessive encounter with its reflection. This has put pressure on the cosmos, like coal being squeezed into a diamond.

4. Over-inflated, mirrored distortions gave the masculine self-importance; the reducing images of the feminine made it feel less – compounded by the shadows cast by unaccessed potential from having to express from limited color ranges, and reduced screen sizes caused by contractions.

5. The way to get out of old ruts has been to reboot the computer – this is done by dumping all old memories and programs. But the computer then reprograms itself. The pineal needs to be reprogrammed not to repeat old cycles through hormones and the bloodstream.

6. Within the screen of life, certain colors should be emphasized to produce through certain qualities, the breaking down of man-made mazes.

7. Three hearts need to become purple: the heart chakra of man, the central crystal, or heart of the Earth (Klanivik) and the cosmos itself.

8. All descension and ascension cycles are to become one. The Hidden Kingdoms are to become physical, staying hidden through magic if they choose.

THE ALCHEMICAL EQUATION TO REMOVE
MAN-MADE MAZES AND REVEAL THE
PERFECTION OF THE LABYRINTHS

Gold = The Courage to Authentically Express

+

Rose Pink = The Flowering of Creativity

+

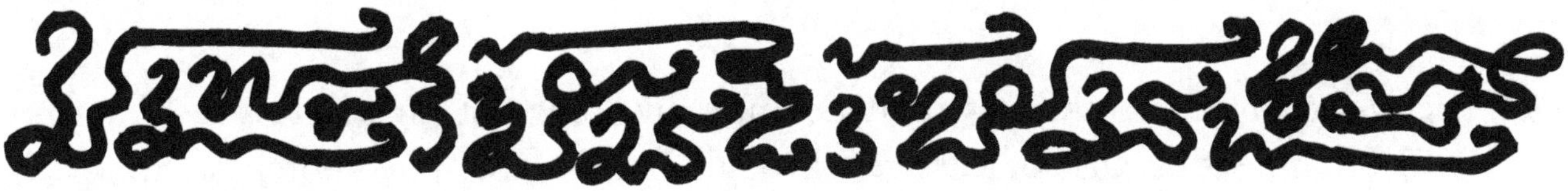

White = The Self-reliance of a Fully Supported Existence

=

The Glad Embracing of the Joyous Adventure of Existence

9. All natures are to become one, by dissolving all previous grids or mazes. Animals will become more conscious.

10. The frontal lobes of humanity are to be fully activated so that images from the Infinite can be clearly seen. The 3rd eye chakra is to be changed to silver.

11. The most recently formed grid of the wolf promotes the desire to create drama. This must be replaced with the quality of peaceful exploration of the self in the adventure of unfolding life. This must be emphasized in the Inner Warrior, Inner Sage, and the masculine (little boy) aspect of the Inner Child.

12. The receiving area for the unaccessed potential is the solar plexus. As we use the imagery of the stories, it grows larger until the receiving area includes the entire body.

13. The third chakra becomes orange. It is a gateway to the potential within. This was obscured before by the grids of the natures, thus we reached for it without the cosmos. There is no within or without.

14. Learning to feed off the new daily potential by going within will reverse aging, which happens because of leakages through 'holes of untapped potential' in the body.

15. The voice of all beings needs to be recalibrated anew all the time, to express newly accessed potential. Combined with new truth, it renews the body. Forgetting what we think we know assists this.

16. When the voice is recalibrated to express accessed potential, it combines with new truth alchemically to break down old matrices and grids, and silences the will of the little, egoic self.

17. The cycles of ascension and descension, and the natures and potentials surrounding the cosmos, are the 4 directions that must combine to birth a life of no opposites.

18. Neither expansion nor contraction exists. It is only the game of changing focus to bring playful variety to the adventure of life.

19. Questions based on a premise of illusions create insecurity and more questions. Questions based on what is indivisible and real, enhance the adventure.

20. The subpersonalities and the masculine and the feminine will always be ill or broken – they are based on separation.

21. The dissolving of separate subpersonalities can only happen when all are equally expressing. The nurturer is expressing but does not feel heard. It can provide the spiritual nourishment we seek without.

22. The feminine's domain is darkness, a black slate that can hold many more colors than a white slate. White light is confined to 3 primary colors. The masculine programs life to fear darkness and value light, ignoring and devaluing the feminine.

23. The mazes, the cycles of life, the natures – all were created as a method of control and security by masculine subpersonalities. The feminine had no part in creating the computer screen. The Labyrinths and yogas were given as keys to get life out of the screen.

24. The ancient contentment of the endless depths, like the ocean we come home to, like the land as old as the Earth: these are the feminine foundations of our being, inviting us through daily communications of imagery and poetry, to get to know it until we live immersed in it. Then we will know we are home.

25. The feminine is the foundation of life – from it, in a series of 3 schisms, the masculine warrior, the elder, and the masculine of the inner child split off. Their activity has seemed like madness to the feminine, which withdrew from it as the masculine went around and around.

Discourse 7
Tolerance of Diversity

Q. There are so many areas of conflict worldwide. How can we as individuals bring tolerance of diversity to the world?

A. That is a masterful question that recognizes the power of the individual to change the world by changing himself. The most important step in changing your environment is to ask, "What do I need to change about myself"?

Q. Why are we intolerant of the conduct and diversity of others?

A. There are multiple reasons. Firstly, when we aren't living our inner subpersonalities, our inner tribe isn't supporting us, in that it is disrupted in its function. We then seek a tribe, by wanting to surround ourselves with others that mirror uniformity and sameness. We reject the diversity of others.

Q. This seems like it's at the root of our intolerance.

A. Yes, tolerance can't be taught when we are intolerant of our own subpersonalities, refusing them expression. Unless this is dealt with from within, even the removal of media programs of intolerance, like racial stereotyping, will only move our intolerance to more subtle forms, such as intolerance of the ideas of others. In the case of lightworkers, there is intolerance for those of less consciousness and awareness, in that we try to save them or fix them.

Q. What are key concepts when dealing with the rest of the world from a highly conscious level of awareness? Everyone else seems to be living lives that make no sense.

A. The two primary realizations in any interaction with others are:

1. Anything that must be said can be said nicely with the development of social skills. We must ask ourselves: Is it true, is it kind, and is it necessary? A difference of opinion becomes a learning opportunity for you when you realize that you have nothing to prove and everything to learn.

2. The second realization is that we leave others better off after an interaction with us, when we truly appreciate and see them, by being interested in them. Others find us interesting, when we are interested in them, to a much larger extent than our wealth, beauty or power can achieve. An interested person is an interesting person.

Q. How do we appreciate them, and how do we learn something from them – for instance, from the shop clerk who is selling us a soda?

A. The answer for both is the same, to some extent. By seeing something praiseworthy in them – the more irritating their lack of excellence is to you, the greater is the more hidden strong suit that waits to be discovered by you…

Q. And, how do we learn from that?

A. We can only ever see something in another that is in ourselves. That is why Toltec mystics teach that all we can ever know is ourselves. Anyone's strong suit that we discover is a revelation about ourselves.

Q. Yesterday I was irritated by the laziness of the attendant pumping gas at the garage. He helped everyone except me. How should I see him?

A. Look deeply at his life, what it would be like to be him, and what has made him work in slow motion.

You will find that he has no hope of ever getting out of the rut of pumping gas, five days a week, to support his family. The pain of his entrapment is reduced by using marijuana. Various drugs, including valium, alter our perception of time. It feels to him like he is working full speed, and to you, as though he's in slow motion. To those who cease to resist life, thought is reduced, and time alters as action becomes automatic. You can live much faster than the rest of the world in that you don't have to pacify reason and you can multi-task.

Secondly, the gas attendant sees his life spreading out in front of him with little or no change. He isn't interested in rushing into such a bland future. He feels powerless to change his life, but the bit of control he can exert by making you wait, at least makes him feel as though he has some power.

Q. So, what have I learned about myself?

A. Look at him again. What you can see is either an ignorant fellow who isn't doing his job well, and is wasting your time. Or, you can see a hero who endures hours on his feet in the rain and wind to feed and clothe his family, but whose steadfast heroism gets no praise. You will see yourself in him. Day by day, you refine and live your highest truth on an eternal, endless journey that has no point of arrival. Your steadfast moral courage, and inner victories, are unsung deeds of heroism none can see, but slowly the world around you is blessed by your courage and steadfastness. The lesson? Give yourself encouragement and approval for moral victories, and step free from the illusion of having limited time.

Q. But people bound by mortality because of the belief system of death have limited time.

A. The more you live from the still point of the surrendered life of trust, the more you master how fast time flows. A moment can last a year or a lifetime.

Q. If I look at why I'm irritable with the way others behave, one reason is that I detest being treated as an idiot.

A. Many who work with the public are following rules set out by employers to deal with all possible eventualities. These rules are meant to deal with people from all levels of life – they're idiot-proof. The fact that they irritate you shows that you have moved beyond the thoughtless masses governed by rules, into a state of self-government. What it's teaching you, is that all cannot conform to your high levels of perception, and that you have to accommodate diversity. When the symphony of life plays, not all notes play at once. Without some of the notes being silent, there would be no music at all. Honor and acknowledge the silent ones, as well as the ones that play.

Q. How far should we take your often repeated admonition to "interact sparingly with the world, otherwise, we deplete ourselves and others"?

A. The more conscious you are, the more empathic you become. Your life is destined for greatness. You are one of the symphony's notes that is playing. If you live your life pretending to be one of the ordinary masses, you will soon believe you are one of them, as you suppress your exceptional qualities in order to fit in and be accepted.

Q. Then what is the solution to being in this world, but not of this world?

A. Firstly, establish your sacred and sovereign space, and way of life – your own reality.

Q. How?

A. All of my writings of many years have been dedicated to providing the tools and knowledge for living a sacred and self-sovereign life. Let every act be an act of devotion, and reverence; let your life become a holy prayer. Honor your body as the timeless vehicle of the eternal expression of Infinite Life.

Q. And how should we relate to others?

A. Our relationships are like the spokes of a wagon wheel. Our evolved reality and sacred life is the hub. Make dedicated times in which you sparingly interact with the tribe of man. To allow the empathy of your heart to persuade you that their reality is your reality, is to enter the world of mirrors – to enter the spokes of the wheel of your world, and forsake the hub that keeps it all together in self-integrity.

Structure designated times in which you interact, and give yourself permission to study them. In doing so, uncover hidden things about yourself.

Q. Why? Is there no other way to learn about myself?

A. They are your blessing and your gift. The biggest threat to a highly evolved being is the inclination to step back into the lower reality because of feeling lonely and isolated. The eagle, flying higher than the other birds, leaves the flock behind on his lonely flight. But he can see the entire landscape, and if he were to pretend to be one of the flocks, they would peck at his feathers in an attempt to reduce him to their lusterless level.

Q. What other threats are there than can cause an evolved being to backslide?

A. Stagnation. If a highly evolved being doesn't interact with others of different levels of perception at all, something that has taken place throughout the ages as enlightened ones withdrew from society into isolated mystery schools – stagnation occurs, and they lose the resources to maintain their advanced levels of awareness. The social stage of tribalism is the most inclined to have stagnation because it seeks sameness, or uniformity. For enlightened ones to withdraw from everyday life, is simply to form another tribe.

Q. How do we express ourselves nicely? Is it an acquired set of social skills?

A. See the information regarding conflict resolution, an excerpt from *Journey to the Heart of God*.

Conflict Resolution

PRELIMINARY STEPS IN DETERMINING
WHETHER CONFLICT EXISTS

Excerpt from *Journey to the Heart of God*

If one is walking a path of impeccability, it is imperative to suspend judgment when some seeming offense or disagreement occurs until we have obtained clarity. For example, some acquaintance hurts our feelings, but we realize that words can mislead. We therefore ask, "What did you mean when you said …?" or "Why do you say such and such?" This is not asked in judgment, for no conclusion has been reached, but rather with an attitude of neutrality.

When we have ascertained the true meaning of what was said through feeling the intent behind the words and getting as much clarity as possible, we can proceed. Does it still bring our hackles up or create a knee-jerk reaction? If it does, we need to ask whether it is important enough to resolve with the other person or is it merely one of our 'buttons' that were pushed in order for us to examine some event in our own life that is waiting to yield its insights and power.

If it is important, however, it needs to be addressed. Here are some guidelines on how to decide what is important enough to merit confrontation:

- When there is hurtful intent or destructiveness.
- When it is injurious to the inner child, disrespectful to the sacred world of the inner sage or belittling to the inner nurturer.
- When it violates our privacy or our sacred space.
- When it violates our mutual agreement or trust or is dishonest inany way.
- When it belittles us or suppresses expressing our individuality or causes us to have to be less than we are.
- When it attempts to manipulate, control or dominate us
- When it criticizes or accuses us.

If it fits into one of the above or a similar scenario, the following approach should be used:

- First of all some basics should be agreed upon and perhaps even written.

- Within our relationships all feelings are valid (meaning we do not criticize someone for feeling a certain way).

- All emotions should find a safe place for expression.

- Phrases such as "You always", "You never" and "Why do you?" (when the latter is not a question but a disguised accusation) should be prohibited.

- Neither words nor emotions should be used to attack or manipulate.

- When someone is in the grip of uncontrollable rage, there should be pre-existing coping mechanisms established. They are to wash their face and hands and engage in strenuous activity (exercise bike, jogging, etc.) to organize their thoughts before expressing them.

- Writing letters that are not dispatched is also a productive form of communication where there are rage issues.

  Feelings must be expressed and a solution proposed by the confronting person. This may have to be done a few times before achieving results. "When you do this, I feel this. Is it possible that in future we can try such and such?"

The appropriate way for the other person to respond is to first make sure they understand. "Are you saying that …?" If they acknowledge that a change in behavior is appropriate, it is advisable to create a backup plan since deep-seated habits are hard to break. "Can we have a secret hand gesture or phrase to remind you when old habits creep in?" or, "Could I pull you aside to remind you?"

If instead the other person starts venting, sit absolutely still and let it run its course until it is spent. Then repeat what you said, always bringing the conversation back to the relevant point. If this does not work, write it out and request a written response within a few days. If this fails to resolve the issue, the four steps of conflict resolution, discussed later in this chapter, are introduced (in writing, if needed).

Should the disagreement persist, there are only three choices remaining:

1. Evaluate whether what you have in common contributes sufficiently to your life for you to continue to put up with the differences. If the differences are more significant, either sever the relationship or be prepared for ongoing discomfort;

2. Flow around the obstacles because the relationship has been determined to be worth saving. Be creative. He embarrasses you in public? Create a private world for your interaction and make as many public appearances as possible alone. It is never a good idea to force round pegs into square holes;

3. Change your attitude. Even if you do the damage control suggested in #2 there are still going to be odd times when the offensive behavior will happen. Lift yourself above the situation like the eagle that flies above the world. Envision yourself sitting in an insulating bubble of pinkish purple light, holding your inner child and talking to it during the occurrence.

It is never to the benefit of indwelling life to accept the unacceptable. It is also eroding to have many 'little' occurrences happen day in and day out. How diligently is the person working on improving him or herself? All these factors must be taken into consideration in coming to a final conclusion. Another helpful tool is to picture enduring this behavior for the next ten years and weigh it against the positive aspects of the relationship.

Conflict Resolution According to the Cosmic Blueprint

As said earlier, it is in the densest levels of Creation where all new knowledge is gained and where life bursts forth in the most astonishing array of diversity in order to maximize the opportunity to successfully fulfill the destiny of all lifeforms and to explore the unknown.

But man is unique among these life forms, inspiring in other races of the cosmos both hope and fear. For man, although steeped in illusion, has the almost unfathomable ability to directly shape the unfoldment of the plan of Creation and within our DNA lies the key to initiate the in-breath of God; to take the cosmos over the edge of Creation from the 'red road' leading away from the heart of God to the 'blue road' that returns.

In order to be the way-showers for the cosmos, we have been created to represent all kingdoms and races and are a synthesis of all that is within Creation. But because Creation is a mirror of the face of God and we are representative of all Creation, we are that which most fully represents the Infinite. It is as though we hold a large piece of mirror in which the Infinite observes itself, while other creations hold much smaller fragments that reflect smaller portions of the image.

But it is also the sacred duty of man to solve all conflicts that have not yet been brought to resolution. In this way we not only evolve awareness but as the microcosm of the macrocosm, we upload our gained insights directly to the Primary Trinity (the I AM). As a result of this increased perception, the Primary Trinity reflects down to the Creative Trinity (the Creator) an altered message as to what needs to be explored through Creation. The Creative Trinity then injects into the higher aspects of Creation (the Trinity of In-Dwelling Life or higher self) a change in the way the purpose of the Infinite must unfold. The Trinity of Materialization consequently changes the way life is shaped within materialization. And in this way man's insights have changed all that is.

But because we are representative of the whole, the divine blueprints of the large picture can also be found underlying all situations of our life, from the most mundane to the seemingly chaotic. Conflict resolution is no different; it mirrors the evolving of awareness through the four Trinities of all that is. It moves from conflict to evolved awareness through the same four distinct stages displayed in the large picture.

THE FOUR STAGES OF CONFLICT RESOLUTION

Stage 1

In the Primary Trinity, the I AM gathers all that is uploaded to it from the insights of our lives, all new information about the mystery of beingness. But within the Infinite the same poles attract and within Creation opposite poles attract. The Primary Trinity therefore attracts all that resonates the same. In other words, it keeps and grows more luminous from that which it recognizes to be the same, namely that which is life-enhancing. The rest is passed on to the Creative Trinity for resolution.

In the first stage of resolution, we find our common ground. Unless this is first identified, we cannot properly determine which parts to resolve in Stage 2. Failure to determine what we have in common with the opposition robs us of the priceless gift of becoming more knowledgeable by learning new aspects and viewpoints of that which we are (common ground). Too often, opponents prematurely focus on the differences during this first stage instead of simply assimilating the commonalities so that these initial gifts of insight can be received.

Stage 2

The Creative Trinity, having received all parts the I AM did not recognize as resonating similarly, now engages in analysis, weighing the unknown pieces against all that has been previously known. Once again it gathers to itself all that can be found to be the same (life-enhancing), examines it in a larger context and isolates that which is different. It now tackles the solving of these unknown pieces through externalizing them through Creation. In this stage of conflict resolution a closer scrutiny of what is the same and what is different must take place. Those unknown pieces must be examined in depth rather than taken at face value to extract common elements. It is necessary to examine these details in the context of the larger picture. Although we may have superficial differences, are we exploring a similar pattern? Are the core issues the same even though our method of dealing with them might be different? In this way the true differences to resolve are isolated from the similarities.

The last step is to creatively externalize them. Design a case scenario and objectively examine the issues as though they are happening to someone else. Reverse roles, honestly examining what it would be like to be in the other person's shoes.

Stage 3

Within the Trinity of Indwelling Life, opposites attract. The known (light) no longer pushes the unknown away, but instead desires to incorporate it within. It wants to turn the unknown into the known through experience. For this it needs form and so must create materialization.

In conflict resolution this stage requires that we abandon our preoccupation with our own viewpoint and genuinely try to understand the opposing position. The need now arises to create a situation to test the validity of the opposing viewpoint; to see and understand it better by observing it in action. Where the stakes are high, the testing of the unknown can be done in multiple, smaller controlled settings.

Your teenager wants to date. You feel she's too young, she feels you're ruining her life because all her friends date. After completing the previous steps, one or two controlled situations could be tested wherein she is dropped off and picked up by you and has to call you if she changes locations. This option is opposed to one requiring an absolute yes or no with one party or the other feeling unheard. An informed conclusion can then be drawn as to what can be supported.

Stage 4

In the Trinity of Materialization, the unknown is incorporated into the known through experience. The previously unknown parts of the Infinite's being become known through our experiencing them and taking the time to gain the insights those experiences yield. New knowledge is gained.

In this stage we agree to disagree. The level of interaction is determined by what can be assimilated without being destructive to inner life or without being light and growth repressive. The key element of the success of this stage is to keep supporting the areas of common ground and the growth of all. Examples of the different degrees of interaction that could be allowed are:

- The in-laws don't like you, but they love your wife. Because they show their dislike when around you, you needn't be in their presence often but nevertheless support your spouse being with them as she chooses. If their intent is destructive, such as to break up the marriage, this needs to be clearly identified and the interaction must then be very minimal or terminated depending on the accompanying level of risk;

- If differences are only superficial but the common goals and philosophies are strong, we find we can live closely together or work together while honoring and supporting our diversity within our unity.

As we have moved through these stages, we have encountered the following ways of relating to each other:

- Uniformity–this is the stage of dependence on sameness to understand ourselves more fully.

- Exploring sameness vs. difference–co-dependence is experienced as we find sameness in the differences. We understand ourselves by observing that which we are not.

- Exploring differences–we seek our independence by focusing on that which we are not as mirrored by the other party. We determine whether the relationship is worth proceeding with.

- Unity within diversity–this is the stage of inter-dependence where we cooperate for the good of the common goals, supporting the diversity each contributes.

This final stage is the goal of all life since it provides the greatest opportunity for growth, whereas uniformity slows growth through stagnation. The more differences there are, the more uncomfortable the relationship will be; the greater the commitment to the greater goal, the more stable.

Discourse 8
Finding Meaningful Living

Q. How should we approach *The Poetry of Dreaming* that we learn about in the book you wrote, *Labyrinth of the Moon*?

A. As layers of deep mystery to be explored in humble awareness. The verses are peepholes into eternity.

Q. Please give an example. Can you remember any of the verses?

A. "In horizonless white, a ring of musk oxen, stand alone together"

Q. Please show us the mystery…

A. In the boundlessness of the shoreless ocean of beingness, (the horizonless white of a blizzard), the most primal relationship forms: tribalism (namely, the ring of musk oxen), in order to give a frame of reference for our experience within the immeasurable vastness of existence. It gives insight into why the formation of the tribe is such a primal need. It creates a space (the ring) within which to experience individuation, such as within a family.

Q. What would be the very core, or primary 'ring of experience,' that we draw for ourselves within the vastness?

A. Individuation – that which differentiates our sphere of unique experience from the rest of existence.

Q. How is the ring drawn? What do its boundaries consist of?

A. We adopt our personal identities from others' opinions of us, from our experiences, and so forth. It's just a character that we play on the stage of our individuation, and the personalities we adopt as our masks and costumes.

Q. Apparently, the musk oxen create the ring around the elderly and the young. They face outwards in their protective ring to keep them from getting lost in the blizzard, and to guard them against the wolves. What does this tell us about the mysteries?

A. It tells us why we form personalities – as coping mechanisms, and to protect the fragile parts of ourselves against the winds of adversity.

Q. What fragile parts?

A. To explain, let's look at another ring that we form within our inner space (or psyche): the inner tribe of the subpersonalities. The four subpersonalities' relationships can be described as four concentric rings with the fragile ones inside, just like the musk oxen.

Q. How does this protectiveness play out? Please explain.

A. The inner circle is the person's Inner Child. Around it lies the circle of the Inner Sage (who sees to the well being of the Inner Child by helping it understand why it feels the way that it does, and who listens to the Child). Around the Inner Elder (or Sage) is the ring of the Inner Nurturer, who sees that the needs of the Child and the Elder are met. The outer ring is the Inner Warrior, who faces outwards, making sure that the challenges of the outside world are met, and that no injury comes to the Nurturer, Elder and Child. The personality forms by accentuating different aspects of these different subpersonalities as coping mechanisms.

Q. So, everything we think we are is but a construct of our own making? How can we ever know the self then, who we really are?

A. We cannot hope to ever know ourself, as a being of consciousness as boundless as existence. These tribes of the persona, and the outer tribes, are but an attempt to explore one small fraction of our being. To know ourselves is a never ending journey, like trying to catch the horizon.

Q. There's nothing we can understand that we are? Our understanding is too limited?

A. There is nothing we can understand that we're not.

Q. There are those who search for happiness in pleasure seeking past times. There are those who seek for meaning in there leisure. What should we be seeking for?

A. In the 'horizonless white' of our timeless existence, on an eternal journey that never ends, with no point of arrival, we play games of pretending to know the meaning of life in order to create a reference point within the vastness of our being.

Q. How is the one searching for meaning better off than the one who searches for pleasure?

A. The meaning of life is in truth not to be found. It cannot be assessed from our limited circle, our contracted perspective, whether there even is one.

Relationship of Sub-personalities

WITHIN SOCIAL STRUCTURES OR HUMAN PSYCHE

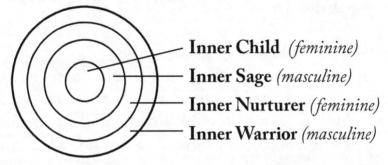

Inner Child *(feminine)*
Inner Sage *(masculine)*
Inner Nurturer *(feminine)*
Inner Warrior *(masculine)*

Each circle is responsible for overseeing the welfare of the circle(s) within it.

THE ROUTE OF COMMUNICATION
BETWEEN THE SUB-PERSONALITIES

Inner Warrior

- Receives interpretation of non-cognitive feelings from Inner Sage
- Communicates to Inner Nurturer when it is safe for vulnerable parts to express and creates strategy for the inner family

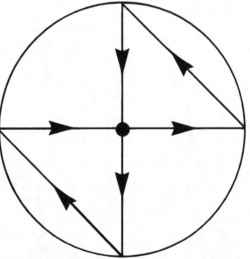

Inner Child

- Expresses its unanalyzed feelings to Inner Sage
- Receives parenting from Inner Nurturer and its dreaming impressions

Inner Sage

- Receives Inner Child's feelings and interprets them
- Communicates deductions to Inner Warrior to act upon

Inner Nurturer

- Receives information from Inner Warrior as to when Inner Child can express and strategy for inner family
- Communicates with Inner Child in a loving parental role

Q. Then why not abandon our striving for mastery? Why is it any better than the hedonistic search for pleasure?

A. The lucid dreamer can determine the quality of his dream better. The more clarity we attain, the more we determine the quality of our journey. Thus, it is not for meaning that we should search for, but clarity.

Q. And the one who searches for pleasure?

A. Such a one cannot control the quality of his reality, he is too immersed in the dream. But, he can control his response to that which he encounters on the journey. It is not for pleasure that we should search, for it fades like shadows before the sun. It is for deep contentment, which is the result of absolute surrendered trust in the fact that our being is the benevolent provider of our sustenance.

Q. Where is surrendered trust to be found?

A. Look not behind you, lest you define yourself by dreams that once existed. Look not forward, lest you abandon the moment in your goal-oriented haste. For it is in the moment, intimately experienced through the eyes of a child, that it is found.

Discourse 9
The Significance of the Individual

Q. The Earth is a tiny dot in the Milky Way galaxy. Our galaxy is one of the billions that are visible to us – with the billions of people on Earth, how can we find significance to our existence within all this vastness?

A. It is daunting I confess, if one looks at it mathematically. The problem is that we are basing all of this on the flawed premise that mathematics is an irrevocable fact of life in all realities.

Q. Well, can you show me any example of where it is not?

A. Yes. In the second week of November, 1996, when the fairy realms opened their doors to me and the *Arubafarina* book was written, the fairies tried to give me information which I wouldn't write because it was mathematically unsound. "Everyone knows 8 + 8 is sixteen and not 54," I argued with them. "I'd lose credibility!" I explained. They just shook their heads and said, "You will learn".

Q. Well, did you?

A. Yes, when the angels gave me the body of information of alchemy, I realized that mathematical results could be leveraged, depending on what it is that you're adding together. Eight plus eight components could be leveraged to 54 (like lead turning to gold), depending on the nature of the components, and the alchemy of adding them together.

Q. Is there another example?

A. Yes, in geometry. During a week in Kent, star beings gave me a geometry that they called, "dynamic geometry". The geometry has no angles or joints; something I would have thought to be an impossibility. But, it takes into consideration the fractal qualities of light and its compulsion to eventually return to its Source.

Dynamic Geometry

The geometric models we use to explain cosmic evolution and relationships use the static, illusion-based geometry of this density. We depend on platonic solids and geometry with angles and joints to get our point across. Within the true geometry of the cosmos such things do not exist.

There are no static objects in life. Everything is part of the great flow of the river of outpouring life, and light flows in a way that has no angles and no joints. The angles and joints are part of the illusion. Light flows in a way that incorporates all our platonic shapes, but it is simply a trick of the eye.

For example, set up two pencils attached in the following way to the edge of a table: the first pencil stands straight up from the edge of the table at a 90 degree angle. The next pencil is attached to the top of the first pencil also at a 90 degree angle to the other pencil, but facing more towards you (i.e., sticking out over the edge of the table). If you now stand above your construction, it appears that the top pencil is in fact touching the table in a perfect triangle. (See image, *The Way Dynamic Geometry Works*.)

Another example is the bottom of the creational triangle. It represents the cosmos and is not flat, but rather the bottom of a figure eight in the interrelationship of its various components. If we depict just the bottom of the figure eight, we would draw the zero point circle and two downward pointing triangles to illustrate the two trinities within created life. If we use a dark enough marker, and fold our paper over so that the circle of the zero point lines up with the lowest circle, we can see a star tetrahedron if we hold our paper against the light. It appears to have touching edges and joints, even though the triangles are not even on the same plane.

Light bounces off barriers or fields (such as the edge of the space designated for this outbreath of God) in a way that gives them the appearance of a solid shape even though they are not.

Although further and deeper information is given as footnoted, we mention it here so that the reader is aware that the illustrations given represent relationships only and should not be taken at face value.

In dynamic geometry one shape changes into another in one continuous flow.

"Truth is needed first, and where it is present there love will be also… If you hold your mind on the good news of how you and I relate, how we are inseparably one… Understanding will fill your mind with a vision so beautiful, so desirable, so attainable, that you will never have to try to love me. Love will flood your mind and heart spontaneously every time you think of this great vision."

* From the *Door of Everything* by Ruby Nelson.

THE WAY DYNAMIC GEOMETRY WORKS

Example A

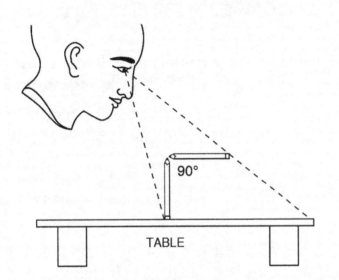

90°

TABLE

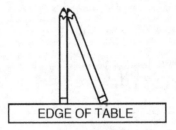

EDGE OF TABLE

To the eye it appears like a triangle even though objects aren't on the same plane.

Example B

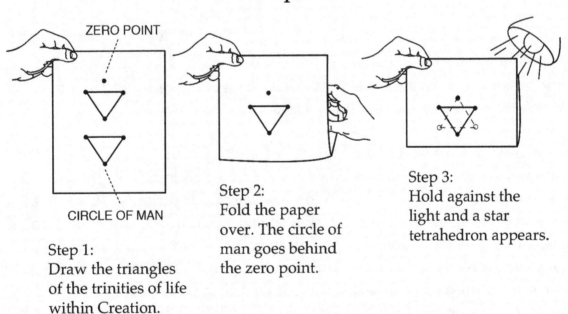

ZERO POINT

CIRCLE OF MAN

Step 1:
Draw the triangles of the trinities of life within Creation.

Step 2:
Fold the paper over. The circle of man goes behind the zero point.

Step 3:
Hold against the light and a star tetrahedron appears.

Geometric shapes appearing as having angles and joints are but a trick of the eye.

Q. How does this apply to the significance of the one?

A. Firstly, it loosens the grip of previous belief systems, enabling us to ask, "What if" questions.

- What if math as we know it didn't exist? Would we still think that the one has less value than the many?

- What if we consider that the one and the many are the same? That we can only recognize that which is within, thus all we see without is really ourselves?

- What if we live in a mirrored world, the mirrors created by our own belief systems and value judgments? Are we in fact, staring at our trillions of body cells when we look at the galaxies?

Q. So, it enables us to brainstorm and entertain the possibility that all is not as it seems, by keeping a fluid perspective?

A. Another good way to demonstrate the power of the one is to imagine a pipe stretching for miles and completely filled with marbles. If one marble more is inserted on one end, every one of millions of marbles must move, and one falls out the other end.

Every one can affect everyone else with every choice he or she makes – all the marbles must move.

Q. If the one affects the many, and the many affect the one, they are equally powerful no matter what the illusion of mathematical numbers might say?

A. We should also consider that space is an illusion – instead of staring into outer space, we could instead be staring into our inner space.

Q. Can you give us an example of space as an illusion?

A. If you stand between two mirrors, looking forward or backwards over your shoulder, you see many images of yourself (the illusion of numerical superiority). These lines of images create the illusion of linear space even though the mirror is just a flat piece of glass. It would be silly for the one, the person standing between the mirrors to feel insignificant when compared to the greater number of images when he is the source of their existence and they all change with the slighted change, of their source, namely the one. Now, I have a question for you regarding the previous statement you made: "If the one affects the many, and the many affect the one, they are equally powerful…"

Q. Oh, I see! All the mirror images in the world cannot make the one do anything! They have no power at all, but what the one gives them. The many cannot affect the one and outer space is a reflection of inner space. It is ourself that we marvel at when we study the beauty of the galaxies.

A. Exactly!

Q. But what about the self-destructiveness of man, for instance millions of people yearly injecting the neurotoxin Botox into their bodies and other habits of self-loathing? How does that affect the macrocosmic picture?

A. Over the ages there have been a few called 'saints' who have become the source of legends, by being impervious to poison and other life-threatening situations. They do this by realizing that such negativity isn't 'real'. It cannot exist within the benevolent support of eternal life. The negativity we express, called 'sin' by those who wish to control through guilt, is just a dream stemming from those parts of us that are asleep. Our dreams do not affect daily life. Our environment (the mirror images) do not respond to our dreams.

Q. Then, how can anyone be guilty of any misdeed if they are but dreams?

A. They can't. There is only innocence. Our penal system is a failure because it reacts to illusion instead of waking up that part of the 'perpetrator,' better called the 'dreamer'.

Q. What about the theory that the tyrants of man throughout history, have conspired to keep man small, so that they're controllable.

A. If the tyrants truly knew the power of the one, they wouldn't be tyrants.

Q. What do you mean?

A. Who would choose controlling a certain limited group of citizens, over knowing that they can affect the whole world? It's usually deep-seated impotence that turns people into tyrants when they're given a bit of authority.

Q. Also, if we realized the power of the one, there wouldn't be tyrants in our reality because we would use them as indicators that there are tyrants within…

A. Yes, and by eliminating them, they disappear without. Tyrants within could want to live up to other's expectations, or are being subjected to social conditioning.

Discourse 10
Turning Stumbling Blocks into Stepping Stones

Q. Why is there so much aggression on Earth, both among man and in the animal kingdom?

A. Because we misunderstand the nature of life. We see it as hostile and unsupportive, and ourselves as victims of one opposing factor after another.

Q. If life is not hostile, how did we gain such a distorted perspective that sees aggression as a necessary weapon to fight against the hardships of life?

A. By not living one of our inner subpersonalities.

Q. So we have the Inner Child, the Inner Warrior, the Inner Nurturer and the Inner Sage – which is it?

A. No, these are the subpersonalities of the vertical axis of the psyche of man. The horizontal axis consists of the Inner High Priest, also called Wise Woman (or high mind), the Inner Babe and the Inner Wild Woman. The subpersonality that's missing is: the Inner Adventurer or Scout.

Q. How did it go missing?

A. It has a unique role in that it gives three-dimensionality to life; experience becomes more real to the individuation – like being in a virtual reality. When it's dormant, life is experienced like being on a flat two-dimensional television screen that only gives the illusion of depth.

When we started taking life at face value, believing in appearances, the adventure of life was lost; it was only a series of hardships.

Q. Why does nature seem so hostile? For a mouse to walk across the field is hazardous because of all the predators.

A. Nature, specifically the animal kingdom, embodies that subpersonality of the Inner Adventurer for the Earth. If it is unlived by us, the expression in nature will reflect that also.

Q. What subpersonality of the Earth does the plant kingdom represent?

A. The Inner Babe. When we disconnect from Nature through being over-polarized into business in our outer world, plants die because they feel unloved and unappreciated. The Inner Babe is representative of a rich inner world, something we connect with through contemplative introspection, and through beingness rather than doingness. Babies spend the majority of their day in their Inner Space and in inner experiences. The Inner Babe is the connection between Inner and Outer Space.

Q. What viewpoint does the Inner Adventurer offer to deal with the hardships of the world?

A. The essence of manliness, what it means to live up to the often quoted and always misunderstood phrase: "Act like a man". It means that instead of complaining and whining about your circumstances, respond to them with courage born of a change in attitude.

Q. Do women have this aspect too?

A. Absolutely, all are connected the same. Gender is determined by emphases.

Q. What is the attitude change?

A. Everyone has instinctively known there's something missing in the expression of manliness when someone whines and complains. Yet no one has known how to respond to it, except through aggression. Assertiveness and aggression are two entirely different things. Aggression creates more opposition…

Q. Wait a minute…why?

A. Because we strengthen what we oppose. Carefully consider that answer because it holds many hidden truths. The field mouse running across the field for instance, regards the many dangers as, 'life is hard for a little guy like me'. He knows that with the overcoming of each obstacle, he grows more invincible, more self-reliant, and with more wisdom to pass on to the next generation. To him, the field isn't a minefield of danger, but a testing ground that sharpens his senses and hones his survival skill.

Q. Instead of looking back and saying 'life was hard,' we look back and say 'look at what I've overcome'. Our confidence grows and our cynicism diminishes.

A. Yes, and cynicism destroys innocence and innocence is the root of all happiness.

Q. How can one look at something really tragic and think of it as an adventure?

A. Cry your tears, rage if you must, but know that it's a passing adventure of your life. Looking back at the war years, people often have a nostalgic fondness for the fashions of the times and the lifestyle. People can afford to feel nostalgic retrospectively, because they know the outcome. Don't look at what you've suffered, but what you've overcome to gain your present strengths.

Q. What about things you've lost along the way?

A. Whatever you have lost, you manifested in the first place, which means that you can manifest it again. But make sure that it is still your priority. Does what you long for represent an element that has been lost from your daily life? By re-awakening that element, the longing for something in your past may disappear. Our being is our sustenance, and always is the source of our fulfillment.

Q. What about suffering that we do on behalf of others?

A. Martyrdom is as barbaric as the ancient Druid priests slaughtering their kings to appease the Earth Goddess if the weather went out of balance, except in this instance: we sacrifice ourselves.

Make a declaration that you will fulfill life as joyfully and as abundantly as you can, for in showing the world how to be happy, do we fulfill our highest calling.

Q. What directions do these subpersonalites represent?

A. The Inner Babe represents the direction of within, the Inner Scout or Adventurer represents the direction of without, the High Pries or Wise Woman represents the direction of above and the Inner Wild Woman represents the direction of below.

Q. Please discuss the application of the directions of above and below in our lives.

A. The direction of above is the greater vision holder. It is the voice of our conscience. When dysfunctional, the conscience steers us according to social conditioning, and the propriety and value judgments of others. When we live authentically, it can fulfill its true calling as the vision holder. Think of it as the eagle's vision: down in the valley, the scout is trying to reach a certain destination or travel in a certain direction. But, because of all the obstacles, which way to go isn't always clear. With eagle vision, High Priest can guide us through conscience.

Q. And the direction of below?

A. The direction of below has often been feared. Wild Woman is still feared by many. She disregards social conditioning and through her instinctually driven actions, breaks down the grip of programmed and learned behavior. She helps us maintain our freedom from the expectations of the tribes we form, and vitalizes our expressions as we respond to things in our daily lives.

Discourse 11
Beyond Cataclysmic Change

Q. If there's no point of arrival on this endless journey of existence, why are we doing so much self-work and self-refinement? For instance, what benefits are there to overcoming death?

A. Life and death are opposites. As we live and die, and die and live again, we are living in dualism. This creates an existence that is subject to beginnings and endings. Furthermore, a life of opposites guides our actions by giving obstacles. It is the primary cause of victimhood and loss of personal self-sovereignty.

By combining life and death, namely in resurrection, they exist in integrated wholeness. Their unique qualities express as an emphases of expression within the ocean – cooperation between two extremes with smooth transitions and mutual inspiration. The higher the tide, the deeper the ebb tide.

Q. What makes resurrection preferable to ascension?

A. The most major difference is that the nature of our individual reality changes to one of greater depth. Life, death and ascension are the positive (proactive), negative (receptive) and the neutral poles of a two-dimensional existence…

Q. It seems three-dimensional…

A. So does the television screen, which is a flat two-dimensional experience, giving the impression of three-dimensional images.

Q. Where does ascension come into this?

A. It is the center of the child's seesaw, or teeter-totter, in which it takes constant control to keep the motionless balance between the two opposite ends. It cannot be indefinitely maintained without constantly controlling its environment.

Q. Then ascension has to be maintained? It isn't a place of arrival?

A. There is no point of arrival on our timeless journey. But by control of our environment, is this state maintained – it is the reason why ascended masters withdraw from society. The first detriment that occurs is that in trying to maintain its state by suppressing that which it's not – it has created an opposite for itself, and opposites create opposition, as the opposite pole pushes and fights for its place in the sun. Ascension pulls in cataclysmic change. Secondly, the detriment of a neutral pole is that it has to stay motionless and suppress movement. This creates stagnation, and the consequent energy loss ultimately creates death.

Q. But I thought that ascended masters could achieve immortality. Is immortality not then a permanent condition, once its achieved?

A. No. Under the best of circumstances, immortality is but a delaying of death for 10,000 years. Incorruptibility is the mastering of life and death as one.

Q. How does one exist in life and death as one?

A. It is like owning a house but you only live in one room of it (the phase of life). Sometimes you move into a second room and live only there (the phase of death). The other rooms in this four-room house are unfamiliar to you. During the first stage of resurrection, one uses two rooms (life and death), as one wishes, leaving the door between them open.

Q. Are these associated with an emphasis on certain inner sub-personalities?

A. Yes, life emphasizes the Inner Warrior, and death emphasizes the Inner Nurturer. When we ignore self-nurturing, the Inner Warrior goes out of balance and life becomes one big fight.

Q. When do we become familiar with the other two 'rooms' of the psyche?

A. The third room is accessed by emphasis within on the Inner Child, the two layers of subconscious. We learn to live within this room during the second and third stage of resurrection.

Q. So the fourth room is accessed beyond the stage of resurrection? What lies beyond resurrection?

A. I don't know. I haven't traveled there yet, but we can deduce what it's like by studying the microcosm: the psyche of man. It can become accessible by emphasizing the Inner Sage and understanding the depth of its expression.

Q. You had associated resurrection in our earlier discussion with the subpersonality of the Inner Babe. How does this relate to the Inner Child of the psyche?

A. We cannot just balance the expression of the subpersonalities in the external expression, in other words, vis a vis one another. They also must be balanced in their internal expression, as each subpersonality also has within it two opposite poles that must be integrated and mutually supportive. The Inner Child has within it, the Inner Babe as its feminine, more passive pole. The Inner Nurturer has the Wild Woman archetype as its more feminine pole, while the Inner Warrior has the Inner Scout (or Adventurer) as its feminine, inner component. The Inner Sage has the Inner High Priest, or High Mind as its feminine component.

Q. The feminine inner components of the subpersonalities sound more passive, except for the Wild Woman. Doesn't it behave proactively?

A. You should perhaps look at 'feminine' as that which receives inner guidance and passes it on to its masculine counterpart.

Q. But you have spoken before of the unfettered and free 'dance' of Wild Woman?

A. The unbounded actions of Wild Woman peeks through our daily actions, the way a red petticoat peeks from under a black dress. It is simply the language through which this archetype communicates the inner stirrings of inspired passion that she feels.

Q. So how does it change life beneficially to express the fullness of the psyche? This abundance of components must surely bring great benefits to life.

A. Yes, it does. It brings dynamic balance within and without.

Q. Explain please.

A. Inner balance creates a stable foundation. Our ups and downs don't drag us along on a roller coaster ride. We feel them, but observe what we feel from an eternal vantage point. Our experiences don't sink us emotionally anymore.

Q. And externally?

A. As we reduce the gap between opposites, change comes with grace rather than through cataclysms. Water that is falling from very high, to very low, falls very forcefully. If the height difference isn't very big, it flows gracefully.

Q. Change is analyzed as going through three distinct stages in the book *Journey to the Heart of God*. How is it different, when opposites express simultaneously?

A. The three stages described as transformation, transmutation and transfiguration, are all part of the dual life we describe as two-dimensional: Life on the flat screen, giving the appearance of depth perception. Change in the resurrected life (as though experiencing a three-dimensional, virtual reality) is done through transcendence: spontaneous evolution.

Q. Can you give me an example of transcendence?

A. One reality changing to another without endings or beginnings, like winter turning into spring spontaneously.

Q. How can spring, in this limited example, be considered as 'evolution'?

A. It is an example, that is of course taken out of context (spring changing into winter again makes it a cyclical experience), but spring can be regarded as evolution of our external experience of life, because it offers increased, external sensory experiences, and more opportunities for manifested life to flourish. Winter can evolve our inner life if we take time for beingness.

Q. Why are there not more examples of transcendence in life around us? What about butterflies forming from caterpillars?

A. Life on Earth has just recently had the opportunity to resurrect, as the Earth itself resurrected. The change from caterpillar to butterfly is transfiguration: One form is eliminated for another. A tadpole becoming a frog would be a better example of transcendence, since the tadpoles' body doesn't perish, but evolves without cessation of life, into a more complex form of individuated expression.

Q. Why did we previously have large planetary cataclysms?

A. The Earth has tried several times before to make the leap to resurrection but has failed. The totem of Bear tells us why: "Nature has not been purified and evolved as it should have been since the planetary ascension began."

Q. Why was nature lagging behind?

A. Because the Inner Scout or Adventurer became dormant when the unknown was regarded as 'unsafe'. Man started to try and control life rather than see that through its adventures into the unknown, new potential floods in. This kept nature in a less evolved state, parts of it didn't evolve and express.

Q. Didn't that leave gaps in the tapestry of life?

A. Existence does not tolerate holes or vacuums. So man became more animalistic and started to express traits that animals should have been expressing, not an evolved human.

The Wisdom of the Totem Animals of the Cycles

EXCERPT FROM *Labyrinth of the Moon*

Dream Symbols Pertaining to Incarnational Cycles

Creational cycles each produce a specific challenge in order to arrive at their unique perception. The totem animals of these cycles of life will appear, when it is time to live their particular insight. Aggressive behavior from these animals in the dream further indicates an extreme urgency to grasp and apply their perception to avoid unpleasant lessons.

Transmission from the Hidden Planet Minut

The animals embody the stages of the Dream
Twenty-four cycles of life that through eons have been
They are not gone, they linger still
Until their value is seen, they always will
They taint the present and perpetuate the past
As long as they aren't balanced their influence will last
The animals bring the lessons they've carried through time
Each carries a message from ages long declined
Learn their insights that old cycles may disappear
That old programs controlling the present may be cleared

The Totem Animals of the Cycles

1. Unach-tu-savaa
Big Cats
Ascension is the awakening from a dream within a dream.

2. Nanush-bi-sata
Big Mammals, *i.e.,* elephants
Though the dreams become more lucid, they are still illusion-based.

3. Bishu-neresva
Horse Races
Dreams must be understood for the gifts they bring to heal.

4. Kisu-tere-nu
Antelope and Deer
The dream state and the awakened state are opposite poles.

5. Mishapa-situru
Big Birds, i.e., Ostriches
Anything that can be divided into two poles is not real and eternal.

6. Nestu-hiricsta
Amphibians
Both poles must be valued equally in order to express equally.

7. Kaarit-ersetu-harech
Marsupials, i.e., Kangaroo
Poles that express equally can be combined and cancel each other out.

8. Nechvi-harasat
Lemurs
If all their parts are balanced and equally combined, only beingness remains.

9. Sutuvach-barstu
Apes
The only way to permanently eliminate illusion is through combining its equally expressing poles.

10. Perspa-hisata
Dog Races – except Wolves
All other methods – like transformation, transmutation and transfiguration – will just re-manifest the illusion in higher and higher forms.

11. Mishera-pirerut
Wolves
Two opposite poles that exist cast a shadow, which is space.

12. Runarat-aranuk
Armadillo
The interaction between two poles creates the illusion of movement, which is time.

13. Sunarut-blivavet
Domestic and Smaller Cats
When one pole, such as the physical body, is over-focused
on - its opposite pole, such as the soul, diminishes.

14. Kanavit-erut
Pigs, Cows, Sheep
The opposites of body and soul cast the shadow called
spirit, or individuation.

15. Kuhus-estravit
Snakes and Other Reptiles
The animal archetypes represent the 24 dream cycles that
have taken place.

16. Kenevit-arasvi
Other Mammals
The dream cycles are representative of the 24 hours of the
Earth's rotation.

17. Vrunabit-ruseta
Water Fowl and Poultry
There are 24 levels of dreaming both cosmically and for all
beings.

18. Asanach-vuhesbi
Birds of Prey
The animals carry the dream cycles insights, which must
be learned in order to dissolve them and the illusion of
dreaming and awakening to be cancelled out.

19. Klihes-uspenes
Other Birds
As the cosmos moves to more lucid dreams, old dream cycles do not disappear. They remain as shadows waiting for their value to be seen.

20. Graanit-plubahes
Bears
Nature has not been purified and evolved as it should have been since the planetary ascension began.

21. Visinetvi-araskrut
Marine Life – except Whales
The animals still carry the shadows of previous dream cycles, known as the cycles of the Fall.

22. Arsa-velebruch-nava
Whales and Dolphins
The remnants of the 24 dream cycles have also formed the subconscious of the 24 root races and thus affect cosmic life.

23. Kusabit-eleklutvi
Bees
This creates a past and disturbs cosmic purity by perpetuating memory.

24. Nunusit-plavi
Other Insects and Spiders
Eliminating dreaming and awakening eliminates all cosmic illusions and is the ultimate cosmic alchemical equation.

The Wheel of the Dynamic Balance of the Subpersonalities

Inner Warrior and
Inner Adventurer

Inner Nurturer
and Wild Woman

Inner Sage and
Inner High Mind
(also known as
Inner High Priest)

Inner Child and
Inner Babe

THE SIGIL OF THE FULLY EXPRESSED INNER ADVENTURER (ALSO KNOWN AS THE INNER SCOUT)

Sigil name: Kaarnesh Hisabet Arakve

Quality: To help Nature flourish

Note: For three days, the fragrant smell of wet soil filled my room. It came from an elf sitting in the window box outside my window. He was waiting for this sigil to be drawn, and when it was, he jumped up and down, squeaking with delight.

Discourse 12
Answers to Planetary Anomalies

Q. Strange hairless dogs are showing up in Texas during the last few years. They're hard to catch on film. They've outrun a truck travelling 45 miles per hour. But there is one stuffed specimen. It has blue eyes, two prominent nodules on the rump, two nipples instead of four, and a large skull…not very pleasing to the eye.

A. More new species will be discovered. The cosmos has life and death cycles, two parallel realities with the death cycles containing some extinct animals. As the cosmos has prepared for a resurrected state, these two realities are merging and these animals are entering our reality.

Q. It's been known to kill chickens but not eat them. Why?

A. It firstly represents a dysfunctional quality found in man: senseless and wanton destructiveness. Secondly, it is not fully integrated into our reality and cannot sustain itself on the chicken's flesh. It eats the chicken's soul. After all, it is from the soul of the cosmos, or death realms.

Q. In some towns, hundreds of dead birds have dropped from the sky. What is killing them?

A. Not only do alien UFO's use stealth technology, some miles in diameter, but the United States' Air Force does also. The flocks of birds, some on migration routes, can't see the craft and fly into it, killing themselves from the impact.

Q. Some talk about the non-hostile nature of the Yeti or Bigfoot, others claim they are murderous. Native people of the Americas revere them. Which is it?

A. The confusion arises by not realizing that the Yeti is a different creature than Bigfoot. Let's call Bigfoot (or Sasquatch) by his ancient name, known in Lemuria: "Andazi," which means the wise one. The Yeti is a cruel, carnivorous being, genetically closer to an animal. The Andazi is a totally different evolutionary line, closer to man than an animal. They are herbivorous.

Q. Why do people not discover the skeletal remains of either?

A. Skull pieces of the Yeti have been discovered in Nepal. I don't know where they are located right now, but they have been found.

THE SACRED SOTHIC TRIANGLE

REPRESENTING THE NINE PHASES OF HUMAN EVOLUTION.

STAGES   PHASES

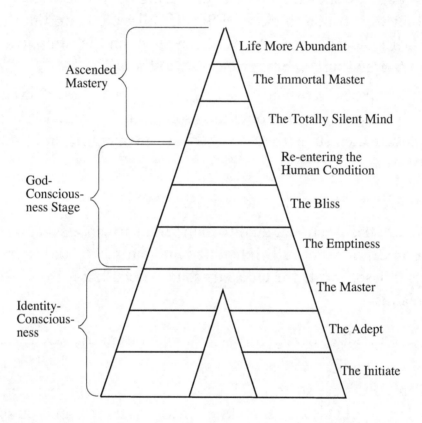

Ascended Mastery
- Life More Abundant
- The Immortal Master
- The Totally Silent Mind

God-Consciousness Stage
- Re-entering the Human Condition
- The Bliss
- The Emptiness

Identity-Consciousness
- The Master
- The Adept
- The Initiate

The Sothic triangle has a 4 to 9 proportion and is also the ancient hieroglyph for Sirius. It represents the secret that the last three gates or phases within Ascended Mastery lead to godhood. The two triangles represent levels of perception as seen by someone at the base of the pyramid (Identity Consciousness) and at the top of the pyramid (Ascended Mastery).

Q. And the Andazi?

A. Buffalo are animals that are in god-consciousness. Hence, certain tribes in North America view them as masters. Andazi don't leave skeletons behind because they are ascended beings. They sidestep the soul world of the dead, and move straight to the ascended master's realms. Most reside there. They take their bodies with them as they move between life and ascension.

Q. Is it a service to the planet that they come to fulfill when they return?

A. No, it's just a preference that makes them come back for the adventure of physical life. Their presence does however bring a gift: a frequency, which is the tone of fortitude. Fortitude is a perspective of minimizing hardship by seeing it against the backdrop of eternal adventure.

Q. Why did indigenous hunters not bump into them more frequently?

A. Because they respect and avoid their territory, which the Andazi mark by planting a tree upside down in the ground – roots to the top.

Q. There is a rumor that Montezuma's treasure is buried in North America. Is that true? And why in North America?

A. Yes, to keep the Spaniards from getting it, 900 slaves with several hundred Aztecs brought the treasure to Utah. It is in a sealed cave on a farm on the outskirts of Kaleb, a small town in the state of Utah.

Q. May I ask, how you know this?

A. In 2006, I worked with six spirits that had various talents that helped me with my work. By 2007, I had developed many of these gifts myself, and they left. They told me about the treasure (possibly the largest in North America) but said that such a powerful curse had been put on it that anyone trying to find it would be killed by the demon guarding it.

Q. How was the curse placed?

A. It was created by: the *blood* of the 900 slaves that carried the treasure and were sacrificed, the *gold*, which there was plenty of, and *emotion*, the terror felt by the slaves during torture.

Q. Why did they bring it to this location?

A. Those who became Aztecs came originally from this area, but migrated when the great genocide broke out on this continent.

Q. Who was the gold for, and how did they expect to find it again?

A. They made a map of their travels that they wanted to hand to the one called Thoth, for him to get the treasure, which they had collected for him. They also created petroglyphs to indicate the spot. He used the gold for black magic purposes and also self-aggrandizement. The treasure is in a cave under a little lake filled with the ghosts of the Aztecs guarding it.

Q. Were they always known as Aztecs? When did they leave the area?

A. No, they were known as Mulekites and left the area shortly after the Great Flood… I'd estimate about six generations after. There was a big massacre of the people in that valley. Their bones were packed into one of the many smaller caves in that area and are still there. The others had left.

Q. There is a rare, copper scroll that was found among the Dead Sea scrolls that gives the location of the Hidden Treasure of King Solomon's Temple. So far, no one has found it. Is it still there?

A. No, it was plundered by a foreign nation. They tortured people to reveal its location. Nobody knew that the copper scroll was obsolete, so it just stayed there with the other scrolls.

Q. For over a month, it rained what looks like blood, in a location in India. Upon analyzing a sample, Indian scientists found that the red rain contains living one-cell organisms, resembling red blood cells. But, whereas all living organisms on Earth duplicate themselves according to a blueprint held in DNA, these cells seem to be duplicating without DNA. There seems to be a danger in having a strange, new life form among us that could replace ours. It was tested at 300 degrees Celsius and it was not destroyed or detrimentally affected.

A. A meteor fell in the same area some days before. It broke up when it entered the atmosphere. These cells are from another planet that broke up and were in the meteor. The cells were held in the clouds until the monsoons came.

Q. Is it a cell that is from a different life form or is the cell the life form? Why is there no DNA?

A. Etheric beings like angels or devas are formed from cells like that and they duplicate according to a racial blueprint, not according to a DNA blueprint. They are one-hearted and of group mind, and made of etheric matter that can live even in a sun.

VITRUVIAN MAN

LEONARDO DA VINCI

Q. Are they hostile to Earth species?

A. The cells have radioactivity in their outer membrane and the red rain should be avoided. But the beings that can form from these cells are devas, or lesser angels. They are benign.

Q. Most alien interference and abductions happen along a specific latitude in the United States. It has become known as the paranormal highway. Why is this?

A. That latitude, relevant to the body of the Earth, is similar to the nipples on a human body in the Northern Hemisphere, and relevant to the knees if it's in the Southern Hemisphere. On planets, that is where the most storms (like the big red storm on Jupiter) and earthquakes occur. This division is dictated by the geometry of the fields around the body. For alien ships entering the Earth on a designated spot on its timeline (modern days versus the time of the dinosaurs, for instance) it is easier along these two 'highways' in the respective hemispheres. The fields around the body are called the Merkaba.

Q. Is it impossible to find a desired spot in time if a ship enters somewhere else?

A. Not impossible, just more complicated. There has to be a very specific alignment of the Earth, Moon, Sun and the ship. But that alignment changes every day. Some star races use it as a means to date events on Earth. An example can be found at the Denver Airport, dating the day that it was operational. It is depicted by a brass inlay at the entrance.

Q. So these latitudes are like an open door?

A. Once the planet goes into a resurrected state, which it has been doing, its fields, or merkaba, changs and becomes what is known as the god-merkaba. It then becomes self-contained and its two 'highways' close. The same change happens to our merkaba when we balance the directions, or subpersonalities, as we prepare for and enter the resurrected state.

THE MERKABA OF THE HUMAN LEVEL OF EVOLUTION

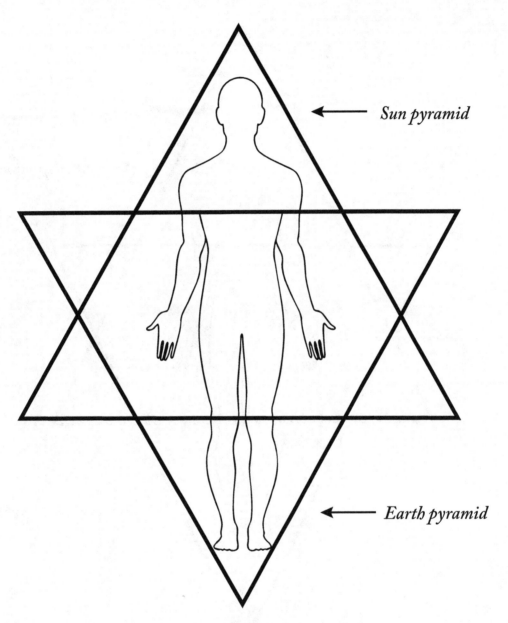

Sun pyramid

Earth pyramid

*Two equilateral
three-sided pyramids,
overlapping from the
knees to the nipples.*

THE MERKABA OF THE GOD LEVEL OF EVOLUTION

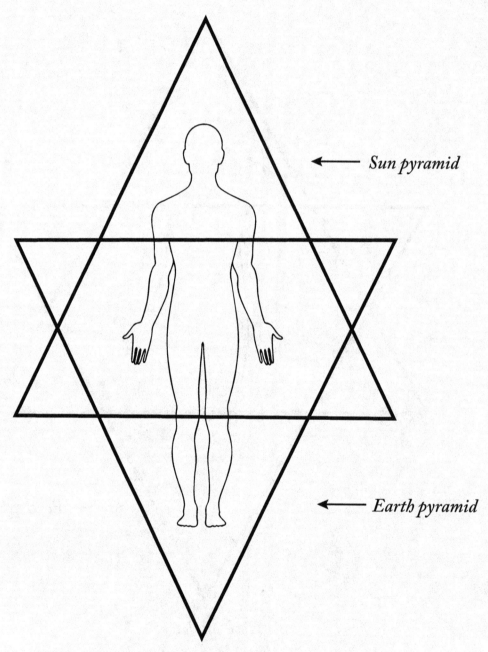

← *Sun pyramid*

← *Earth pyramid*

*There are three star-tetrahedrons occupying
the same space. One spinning left (+), one
spinning right (–) and one stationary (+–).*

*The sides of the pyramid elongate to the shape
of the sothic triangle.*

Discourse 13
The Two Types of Martyrdom

Q. You spoke in our last discourse about keeping beings from the Hidden Realms out of your house, like the little elf in the window box. When one forbids beings from entering their living space, can they still send emotional disturbances into the house?

A. Yes, that has to be shielded against as a separate issue. Generate a strong, positive emotion like deep contentment, and see it expand as a fuschia colored-bubble around the house and declare that no emotions from other sources may enter the property.

Q. How will one know when this is needed?

A. For instance, yesterday I was very bewildered by the rage and irritation of my family members and struggled to keep my emotional balance, and to remain in my inner peace. It seemed like an unusual event and I could see two beings above the house during meditation – an angel, and a Sasquatch or Andazi. The latter was very angry and he was beaming rage into the house. During the night, I asked him what the matter was, after shielding the house. He explained that the Earth was on the brink of losing its balance and tilting onto its axis.

Q. Was this related to your struggling to keep your emotional balance?

A. Yes, and it so happens that after having suffered an injury to the cerebellum, I've been struggling to keep my balance when I walk. So, yes I was struggling to keep my balance on all fronts.

Q. This begs two questions: Why is the Earth's balance in jeopardy? And why are you still doing martyrdom when you call it 'barbaric'?

A. Well, firstly there are two types of martyrdom. The type I called 'barbaric' is the sacrificial lamb type. One person goes through suffering by proxy so that others don't have to…

Q. An example?

A. The Christian interpretation of the crucifixion: an innocent person suffers so others don't have to. This creates a feeling of guilt in the masses, which makes them controllable. Druid priests killed the king so the weather would balance.

Q. And the other type of martyrdom?

A. To learn lessons and gain insights through inner overcoming, in order for reality to change for everyone. This gifts perception, and evolves reality for the many through the evolution of consciousness of the one. This is still a very effective way to bring graceful change to the environment. The perceptions gained by all involved, create a balanced and stable change of reality.

Q. Why is the Earth at risk of tilting?

A. For the same reason that it has always experienced axis tilts: when a critical mass of black magic has been done, it is knocked off balance, creating winds of about 300 miles per hour that flatten most of all man-made structures and wipe out civilizations. Under the snow on Anartica, is a geologist's dream. An entire civilization lived on that land mass before an Earth tilt displaced it to its current location.

Q. Please define black magic.

A. Practices deliberately done to control others and enforce individual will (or the agenda of the few) on the many, or on specific others, or manipulating outcome.

Q. What tilted the scale of life on Earth into the danger zone?

A. The answer is also the answer as to what is causing the "Seneca Guns," or loud booms that shake the houses in New York state, and in other locations on the planet such as India. I've described the population of the hollow, inner Earth in *Secrets of the Hidden Realms*. The ruling class has been a relatively small number of giants. Two opposing giant dynasties are fighting for control at this time. One side, the Oxanohin Clan, has made a deal with a group of aliens from the Antares system to deliver large amounts of gold in exchange for having them mind control the minds of the people to support their bid for rulership.

Q. Are you saying the loud booms are the result of giants from the Inner Earth mining gold from within the Earth's crust?

A. Yes, according to the Sasquatch it is the case, and also the reason for his rage, since they are aware that their explosions and mining techniques are endangered the stability of the planet's axis.

MAPS OF THE INNER EARTH BEFORE 20 YEARS AGO

Excerpt from *Secrets of the Hidden Realms*

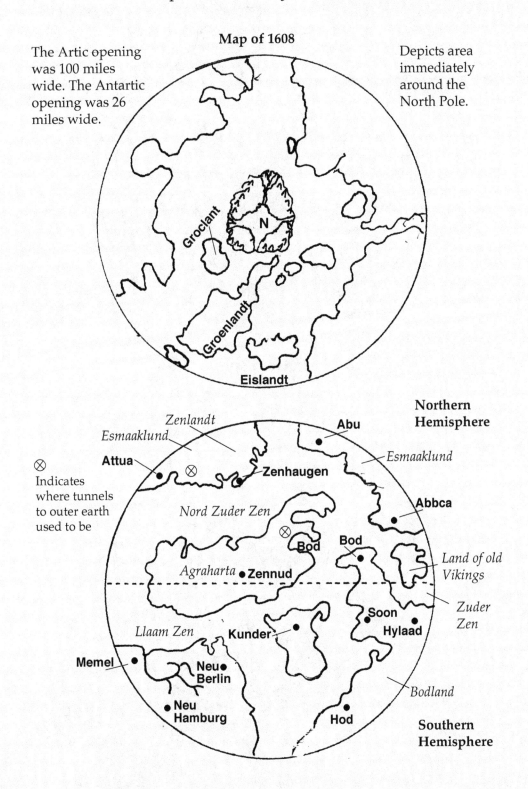

Map of 1608

The Artic opening was 100 miles wide. The Antartic opening was 26 miles wide.

Depicts area immediately around the North Pole.

⊗

Indicates where tunnels to outer earth used to be

MAPS OF THE INNER EARTH AFTER 20 YEARS AGO

Southern Hemisphere View

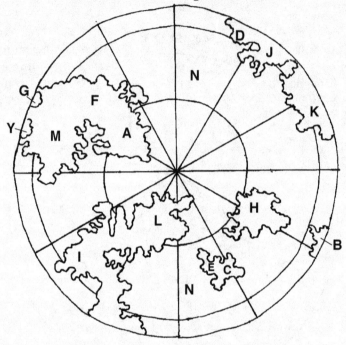

Northern Hemisphere View

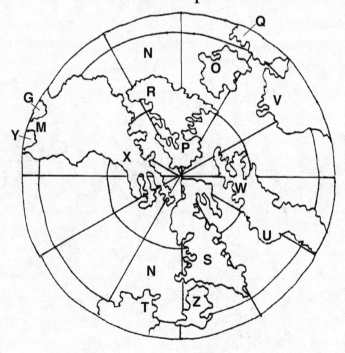

Geographical Names of the Inner Earth

SOUTHERN HEMISPHERE VIEW

A – Hervingenstadt

B – Pelengrud

C – Gelshpi

D – Sparendoch

E – Nor

F – Brepski

G – Ur

H – Hetva

I – Nenhursva

J – Peleursk

K – Vrilsk (Vrilsk is the land of the giants.)

L – Netvi

M – Skrubahirk

NORTHERN HEMISPHERE VIEW

N – Klarenmeer (Ocean)

O – Baringnud

P – Peleninsk

Q– Harsklutva

R – Trechvarutski

S – Trechbar

T – Hurenepski

U – Gruag

V – Balaur

W– Kranuch

X – Rurbahurch

Y – Elvi

Z – Pruchba

The Most Accurate Calendar on Earth

EXCERPT FROM *Secrets of the Hidden Realms*

To understand the Atlantean calendar, we must understand the meaning and great significance of a day out of time. Since we cannot see the vastness of the etheric realms, nine-tenths of existence is unknown.

Before the last sinking of Atlantis dropped the consciousness of man, much more of the unseen realms were as real as the seen. The etheric realms are where materialization begins and it is the etheric that moves through all things, giving life to matter. If something in the etheric changes, it will also change in manifested life unless we prevent it by clinging to our illusion-based belief systems.

A day out of time is a day that exists in the etheric, but not in the physical (though it seems it does to those who cannot see the difference). It is therefore a day that presents the golden opportunity to change aspects of manifested life by changing them in the etheric.

On the Atlantean calendar there are five days out of time; September 23, December 21, January 21 March 23 and June 21. To illustrate this, imagine 365 soldiers standing in a line. If 5 take a step back, there would still be a lineup but those soldiers, like those 5 days, would be on a different plane. (See Atlantean Calendar and Key to the Atlantean Calendar.)

CURRENT USE

As we have noted, the largest population group lives in the inner earth. This Atlantean calendar is the one that they use, making it the most widely used calendar on earth. It is able to indicate time to within 5 minutes.

But, how can a world that cannot see an earthly rotation with its passages of day and night know when a 24-hour day has passed? It is because the inner 'smoky' sun pulses ever 24 hours. Complete darkness is unknown in this inner realm, but a 12-hour period of dimming and another of brightening mark the days and nights.

FEATURES OF THE CALENDAR

The Atlantean calendar has 12 months of 28 days each and a thirteenth one with 29 days. Five of these days are days out of time. As a more conscious civilization living in eternal time, the Atlanteans mapped out frequency segments for use in their daily lives. There is a big change in the frequency of the day every 8 hours, marking a dramatic shift in the frequency 3 times within any given day or 24-hour period.

The 8-hour segments represented polarity, in that one 8 hour segment is positive and therefore a time to be proactive; one is negative and a time to be receptive, and one is neutral in that it is positive and negative. The calendar is so accurate it can indicate exactly during which segment of the day, or the frequency band of the day, an event occurred.

Within each of the three 8-hour segments or frequency bands, 8 one-hour segments form mini bands with more subtle frequency changes. Structuring life to cooperate with the frequency of every given hour was a way of life to the ancient Atlantean civilizations, as it is to the people of the inner earth. Like the changes they noted in birdsong as these frequency bands transitioned from one to the other, their music was composed to balance and enhance each hour of the day.

The smaller one-hour frequency time periods were also mapped out on the calendar and by indicating during which part of the one-hour mini band an event happened, the calendar could place it to within 5 minutes.

The thirteen months are arranged in a circle of twelve with the thirteenth in the center. There are many hidden truths behind a thirteen-month calendar: The number 13 stands for the goddess or feminine principle that gives birth. Time is, in actual fact, the movement of awareness and the movement aspect of the cosmos is feminine. Hence time is feminine.

Time is the birthplace of potentiality into actuality. Thirteen always has the potential to birth something new. In conception, at least 12 sperm must pummel the ovum so that the 13th can enter. In being born into God-consciousness, the twelve archetypal god and goddess facets of the surface mind blend, so the 13th goddess can open the doorway within mind to birth the expanded state of awareness called God-consciousness[*]

The 13th month is positioned within for another reason. It is the month that marks the end of a year—a time for evaluation and introspection. In this way the past year's lessons are incorporated into formulating the desired changes that must be put into effect during the new year.

---

[*] See *Journey to the Heart of God.*

THE MONTHS WERE NAMED FOR
THE GODDESS ARCHETYPES†

Number of the Month Goddess Archetype

1st Pana-tura
2nd Ama-terra-su
3rd Ka-li-ma
4th Ori-ka-la
5th Au-ba-ri
6th Hay-hu-ka
7th Ishana-ma
8th Apara-tura
9th Hay-leem-a
10th Ur-u-ama
11th Amaraku
12th Alu-mi-na
13th Ara-ka-na

The days were indicated by a ring of dots: the first day of each of the 13 months around the ring were marked by a different color dot (color is tone or frequency made visible.) Each of the first 12 months has a tone and color. The 13th month is represented by a 'hole' or portal, indicating that it is a passage to new consciousness.

The days out of time are marked with a separate ring indicating not only that they exist as a separate reality, but also their exact placement in relation to the regular days.

The year is written on a separate part of the calendar in Atlantean. Atlantean is written from right to left, and so the numbers read from right to left.

HOW TO INDICATE TIME

To indicate a specific date (the way we would circle a date on our calendar), a line is drawn from one of the days, or dots, on the outer or second outer ring, depending whether it is a day out of time or a regular day. For example, if it's the 7th day of a specific month, one would count the colored dot, indicating that month, as one and then count six more dots in a clockwise direction. That's where the line begins. The line then moves through one of the corresponding goddess symbols to show at a glance the goddess archetype governing that month.

---

† For the qualities of the months, see the qualities of the goddesses in Part I of this book *(Secrets of the Hidden Realms)*.

If it's the 12th month of Amaraku, it is a time of testing our worthiness and a time to celebrate our achievements. It is a time of bringing closure to our unfinished projects and to prepare for the 13th month of introspection and rebirth—the month of Ara-ka-na that lies ahead.

The line next goes to the day of the week we want to indicate. The seven days of the week were named after the seven lords of light who dwell in the Halls of Amenti. (See the Seven Lords of Light, *Secrets of the Hidden Realms*.)

Monday - Untanas
Tuesday - Quertas
Wednesday - Chietal
Thursday - Goyana
Friday - Huertal
Saturday - Semveta
Sunday - Ardal

The line next indicated in which 8-hour segment the event occurred. But we find the 8-hour segments progressing counter-clockwise. The section of Yod is the 8-hour period from midnight to 8 am. The section of Hay is from 8 am to 4 pm. The section of Vau is from 4 pm to midnight. The counter-clockwise progression represents the structure (or masculine pole) of time, the windows through which time flows.

There are deeper, esoteric meanings about the core of the calendar progressing backwards, or counter-clockwise. One reminds us that time can flow backwards and that certain portions of history were actually lived backwards. Humans appeared on this page of creation, in this loop of time, at a given time. Other cultures actually lived backwards in time, extending history backwards.

In the God kingdom there is a constant feeling of déjà vu in that the next minute is remembered as the past. To decide what to choose, one looks back at the past to see what has already been chosen. It's as though the time of the gods is backwards. This therefore represented the time of the gods.

We then draw a line to one of the spider symbol's (Ara-ka-na's symbol) eight legs. This indicates which hour segment we are talking about. The right hand upper leg (see illustration) marks the first hour and, proceeding in a clockwise manner, the subsequent legs mark the other 7 hours.

Each leg of the spider, however, has 3 segments to indicate in which 20-minute segment an event happened. Each segment can be divided into quarters, to place the event within 5 minutes. The crossover point of the spider's body (drawn as a figure eight), is the eternal now. The line always ends there, reminding us that time is illusory in nature and the eternal now, the moment, is all that exists.

UNDERSTANDING TIME

We need a lot of humility as we approach this very complex subject of time. We know a mere fraction of how time flows. It is the movement of awareness and as such can travel in any direction – and yet we have assumed that we understand it.

Scientists have puzzled about where Sumeria, a complex and advanced civilization, could have originated since it didn't seem to have evolved from previously known civilizations. The actual truth about it, as explained by one of the goddesses, is that it is the result of a 'backwards' evolution of time that occurred as follows:

- Life doesn't occur in trillions and trillions of years of one uninterrupted story. Instead, a series of stories or short plays on the stage of life are designed to explore through life's experiences the unknown portions of beingness. These are called 'pages'. When we emerge on a new page with a whole new stage set, play and sometimes characters, we have no history on that page.

- To make life seem as though it has existed for a long time on that page, some of the characters or civilizations live backwards on an accelerated timeline. For example, if we emerged onto this page, for what us seems like 200 years, but other civilizations could have traveled backwards 3,000 years during the same time period, giving us an apparent history. Otherwise, everything would just be blank prior to 200 years…

ATLANTEAN CALENDAR

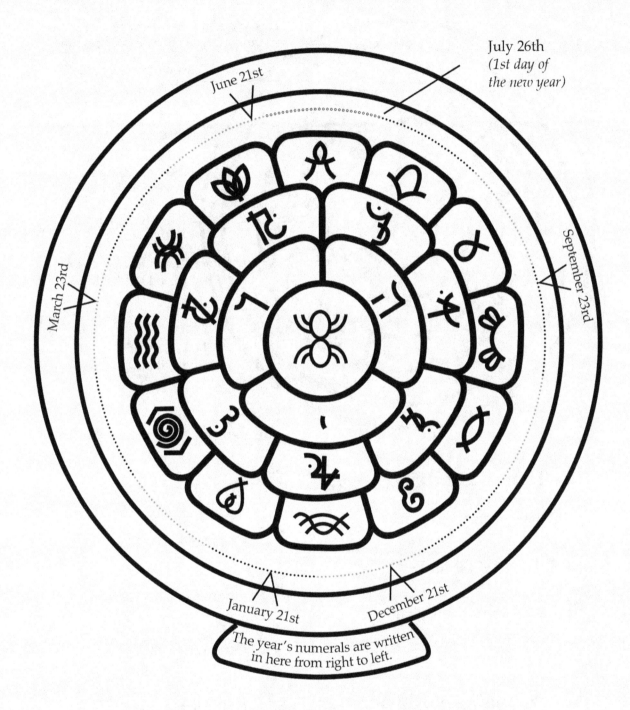

July 26th
(1st day of the new year)

June 21st

September 23rd

March 23rd

January 21st

December 21st

The year's numerals are written in here from right to left.

The days of the 13th month have no color but were indicated by holes or indentions. This signifies that the month functions as a portal to a new spiral of consciousness. The Atlantean year count began after the major catastrophe of 75,000 years ago

KEY TO THE ATLANTEAN CALENDAR

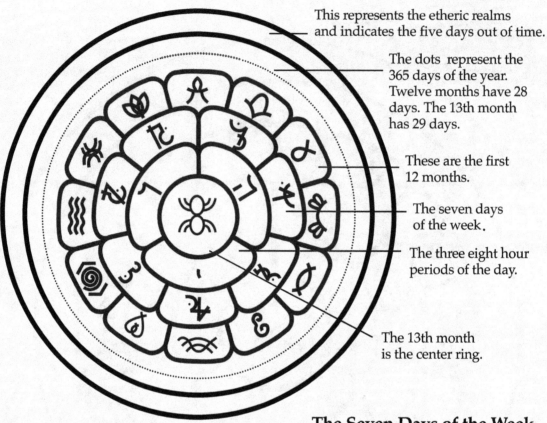

This represents the etheric realms and indicates the five days out of time.

The dots represent the 365 days of the year. Twelve months have 28 days. The 13th month has 29 days.

These are the first 12 months.

The seven days of the week.

The three eight hour periods of the day.

The 13th month is the center ring.

The Three Eight Hour Periods

❯ **Yod** = midnight to 8 a.m.

❯ **Hay** = 8 a.m. to 4 p.m.

❯ **Vau** = 4 p.m. to midnight

Understanding the Spider

The eight legs represent the hours within each eight hour segment starting from the upper right hand and proceeding in a clockwise manner.

The Seven Days of the Week

Untanas – Monday

Quertas – Tuesday

Chietal – Wednesday

Goyana – Thursday

Huertal – Friday

Semveta – Saturday

Ardal – Sunday

Q. Didn't you once say that plutonium when brought to the surface also creates an inebriating effect on Earth? The effect of this in modern times must compound the possibility of axis shifts?

A. Nuclear weapons and energy sources have been on Earth for 180,000 years. The Niburians, according to the Sumerian records that have been dug up, first brought them here. The Ark of the Covenant for instance was a radioactive device and according to the scriptures anyone who touched it died. According to the description of how they died (hair falling out and other symptoms), it matches the symptoms describing someone with radiation poisoning.

Q. The archaeologists believe that the Ark of the Covenant is hidden somewhere in the labyrinth tunnels beneath Temple Mount in Jerusalem. Isn't this politically volatile location an undesirable place to hide a potentially explosive nuclear device?

A. In an out of body travel in 2005, I saw the Ark of the Covenant in an underground storage vault with other relics. They had been brought to the Vatican by the Nazis through underground tunnels.

Q. So in summary, the mining on such a large scale is destabilizing the Earth, which we can help by finding a way to keep our own balance as conscious beings in our chaotic world?

A. Yes, but their use of alien technology to control the minds of man is the exercise of black magic that is an even bigger factor. We can make a big difference by consciously, and by proxy, removing and overcoming any tendency to enforce our will and impose our beliefs on others in an attempt to control them.

Discourse 14
Understanding the World Around Us

Q. Why do we have accomplishments along this journey of enlightenment, only to be told by you some time later that we need to accomplish this same thing again?

A. While in duality, we have been going around and around the cosmic wheel, encountering the same unsolved issues but at higher and higher levels of clarity.

Q. So one could say that we've been spiraling around and around, ever higher?

A. Yes.

Q. But where does the spiral lead to?

A. It makes a bigger wheel or loop.

Q. What advantage is there to facing the life experiences of the bigger loop of existence, rather than the small loops of the spiral? Isn't that what enlightenment is: the larger potential, the larger perspective of larger loops as a goal?

A. Yes, that is one way to use the word enlightenment. The advantage of the chicken that leaves the egg, and the butterfly that leaves the cocoon is simple: that not to do so, is to perish. It is the inevitable next step. The second benefit is the increase in the refined enjoyment of life that the butterfly experiences.

Q. Why do you say that an accomplishment is complete, only to strive to complete it again, later on?

A. One reason is that it was as complete as we could accomplish it from the perspective that we had at the time. Encountering it again, we have gained deeper perspectives and can dissolve the next layer of illusion, like peeling an onion.

Q. Is there another reason?

A. Some illusions are multilayered for a very good reason: they are portals out of a smaller loop, or level, of awareness to a larger one. They open up a more evolved expression of life.

Q. How do they do that?

A. Illusion binds up necessary resources needed for expanded awareness. They are like money in the bank that provides resources when needed. The more layers of illusion that have been built up, the more ancient is the core illusion of the original fallacy. To find and dissolve the original illusion, by seeing through its many layers, provides so much energy that the old reality dissolves and we graduate to a more expanded one.

Q. Does the dissolving of any illusion bring increased energy for enhanced consciousness? What if I asked you if the moon landing was faked?

A. Any removal of lies increases energy, but an illusion like that isn't an ancient, multilayered, cosmic one and so provides a small increase…and yes, it was staged with the astronauts in Hollywood. The footage taken on the moon itself was photographed by an unmanned probe that also brought back some moon rocks.

Q. Why did they do this, to save face in the space race? Were they in fact incapable of putting a man on the moon at that time?

A. The entire space race was a farce, a way to introduce humanity to the idea that man can walk on the moon. Both Russian and America had been sending people up to the moon since the early part of the 20th century.

Q. Couldn't they just reveal that? Why the secrecy?

A. It was not within the technological abilities of either government to do so at that time. To reveal that they had done so, they would have to also reveal that aliens had heavily aided them. They received the technical assistance in exchange for allowing human abductions.

Q. Why did the Russians agree to the Americans taking all the glory for the 'first man on the moon,' rather than themselves?

A. It was in exchange for titanium mining rights on the moon. Furthermore, the Americans had the very advanced Hollywood studios to make the landing look believable.

Q. Is this the reason that the space race ended? The purpose of introducing the public to the idea had been accomplished?

A. Yes, and that Russia and America had been established as the two super powers.

Q. There is a global phenomenon that is showing up in photos and videos, called rods. In some instances, they seem like many pillars of light, from small to large. There are also see-through, fast moving ones that are larger than a jumbo jet. They seem almost organic and have diaphanous frills, or frilly, wing-like membranes down their sides that seem to swim through space at lightening speed. What are these?

A. The stationary ones that appear mostly with people in photographs are beings that follow them between dream and awake stages. They live in the crystalized membranes around various levels of life: the Matrix.

Q. What do they want?

A. The currency of the Universe: energy. They are mostly the source of information that allows people to channel, calling themselves Chief Joseph, Archangel Raphael, or any other name that is meaningful to that person. The more attention they are given, by a person becoming dependent on them, the more energy they receive.

Q. But where do they get their information?

A. From the person's own mind itself. They access parts of the person's brain that is being ignored.

Q. So really, instead of accessing these parts themselves, the person relies on an outside source to tell him what he should already know?

A. Exactly.

Q. What about the fast-moving ones that dart through the air? They seem to move in and out of this reality and our ability to see them…

A. We drew those in 2007. They are a group of Kachinas. Ancient Hopi rock drawings depict them as two parallel lines with a zigzag line alongside each of the outer sides. They can be small (approximately six inches) or very large.

Q. Why are the large ones often filmed around nuclear bases?

A. Fairies help flowers grow. Elves help green plants grow. In the same way, these Kachinas have the job of cleaning up radiation.

Q. My understanding is that the Kachinas were off-planet in the Pleiades for many years, with their memory kept alive by some southern North American Indian tribes, until they returned in 2007. Who cleaned up the radiation while they were gone?

A. A special, designated group of fairies did the work, but they aren't able to keep up with the increased radiation of our planet. They just filled the gap.

Q. You have said that the planetary Inner Child represents the fairies and elves, and that their natural home is the purified underworld. What about the Kachinas?

A. They represent the Inner Babe of the planet. Their natural home is the purified under-underworld.

KACHINA FOSSIL

Fossilized remains of the lost Kachina tribe that represent untaintable and unstainable incorruptibility.

Photograph of Kachina fossil by Karen, Washington, USA.

Excerpt from *Arubafarina*

THE KACHINAS — TRIBES OF INNOCENCE
Transmission from the Kachinas

The Flower Beings

Among the Kachinas before life fell
A tribe of beings among us did dwell
They left for Sirius and Arcturus too
When consciousness slept and darkness grew
In stones their fossilized remains are found
Restore them to Earth that their gifts may abound
Purity can be stained, it is therefore illusory
The true Being of the Infinite has incorruptibility
These Kachinas represent this quality
Among man let them and this quality again be seen

Discourse 15
The Alchemist Within

Q. In looking back at the history of man on every continent, it is a story of bloodshed, genocides, and incredible cruelty of one group against another. It is like looking into the heart of darkness. How can man justify his existence if he has such savagery and destructiveness against other species?

A. First of all, we will only perpetuate the past if we regard it as real. Instead, look at it as a dream that allows you to analyze the symbols it contains for their meaning, and then let it go. Don't fixate on the past and don't let it define you.

Secondly, some enlightened ones, such as those who ask these questions, aren't human at all. They are from the god kingdom. They have come in forgetfulness among man in order to restore the pristine, original template of man. As they live pristinely, they will bring back the true nobility of man. The profound effect on the population of the Earth that they are able to bring about is their gift.

Q. It must be painful for them to live amongst, and believe they are part of, such a warlike species.

A. Yes, which is why the perception of the origin of warlike tendencies in man is helpful. Otherwise they lose power and energy from the constant state of shock they find themselves in when confronted with the rage and combativeness of their neighbors.

Q. But surely they get angry too?

A. Anger serves the purpose of breaking up stuck patterns. But when its indiscriminately present, like a part of someone's identifying characteristics, then it becomes destructive and is no longer useful.

Q. You have said in the *Lemurian Science of Peace* that the origin of war is the conflict of the inner masculine and feminine. Is that also the origin of rage?

A. I wouldn't call it the origin of rage, but it is certainly a source of rage.

Q. What is the anger about?

A. The masculine has rage against the feminine because he blames her for his suffering. The masculine controls the electrical, or nervous system of the body. The masculine works on creating order and integrity in a person's life in order to manifest graceful change and a peaceful lifestyle. The language of pain tells us what areas of our life are not in harmony with our highest perception. It demonstrates where our emotions and attitudes are out of step with our perception. Our physical suffering, felt by the nervous system, is thus often the result of the feminine (the emotions) being out of step with our highest vision.

Q. But surely the feminine is trying to live her highest truth?

A. No, she often deliberately creates the drama and confusion of inharmonious attitudes and emotions. This is what causes the inner rage and conflict.

Q. Why does she promote chaos? That is baffling!

A. Yes, it is as baffling to him, as his rage is to her.

Q. Why would she deliberately cause outer pain and discomfort?

A. To deflect attention away from inner discomfort. There is a horribly destructive trend among some of our young people to self-injure through piercing or cutting themselves. The principle is the same. She is so overwhelmed with inner pain that she tries to localize it externally.

Q. If one looks at the physical suffering on the faces of people around the world, who are battling to earn a living, it's hard to believe that inner suffering is more unbearable than external hardship and suffering.

A. Before we proceed with our line of thought, I want to make it clear that hardship and suffering are not synonymous: One can have hardship without suffering.

Q. Why does she find her inner pain so unbearable?

A. The Inner Feminine's reality is what we can call a reality of oneness, of empathic and telepathic connectedness. The masculine reality focuses on separateness within oneness, of individuality and unique individuation. She absorbs empathically the pain of the masses, and if she doesn't understand the unrealness of the past, she also absorbs the pain of the ages.

Q. What can sublimate this dynamic of the Inner Feminine being asked to carry more than she can bear, which results in her pushing it into external expression, the masculine's domain, who is then enraged?

A. The masculine is not only enraged by her deliberately making life for him more difficult, but also because she holds the solution to reducing the pain of both of them, but doesn't do it. So on top of feeling victimized by her, he also feels unsupported.

Q. How can she make not only the world's pain better, but his pain as well?

A. She holds the key to transmutation. Transmutation is the alchemical process by which something of a lower order is changed to a higher order, like lead into gold. When circumstances are overwhelming, the way to deal with it is through alchemy[‡]. The masculine's strong suit is transformation: the discarding of the superfluous and obsolete, so that the core essence of situations is revealed. It's like cleaning clutter out of a house to make it a peaceful dwelling, and one of the reasons that the deliberate chaos she creates infuriates him so.

Q. When the alchemy that you teach is being practiced, there is usually an equation of separate components to produce a leveraged result. What must be done to create this leveraged result that turns pain and suffering into contentment and grace?

A. There are 12 primary goddess archetypes. Living these archetypes[§] in our daily lives brings vitality and happiness. Physically, it helps clear the 12 main meridians[¶], which brings health to the organs of the body. Even when people work very hard, the living of these archetypes can bring deliverance through changing suffering to passion, joy and peace.

[‡] See the online courses, *The Science of Alchemy* and *High Alchemy: Qi Vesta, The Alchemy of the One* on www.alminewisdom.com.

[§] See *Journey to the Heart of God* for additional details about the Goddess Archetypes. Pana-tura is the Mother, who encompasses all of the 12 main goddess archetypes.

[¶] See *Clearing the 12 Main Meridians of the Body* on fragrancealchemy.com.

THE GODDESS ARCHETYPES (12 ORIGINAL)

1		PANA-TURA Goddess of germination: the Mother. She is the essence of life-giving energy that births into form. She midwifes potentialities into materialization.
2		AMA-TERRA-SU Goddess of history. On earth she is the keeper of the history stored in the rocks, sand, and soil. She keeps the record of the loop of time, which is our biggest history.
3		KA-LI-MA Goddess of equity and destroyer of illusion. She brings balance by creating potentialities that can compensate for distortions that create karma.
4		ORI-KA-LA Goddess of prophecy with the farseeing eye. She is the oracle and holder of the key to changing the future.
5		AU-BA-RI Goddess of sound or frequency. She utilizes the rage of Lucifer to break up stagnant portions of Creation. She is the cosmic sound healer who works with the potential manifestation the spoken word creates.
6		HAY-HU-KA Goddess of reversal energy. She works with indwelling life's purpose to evolve awareness, through manipulating the outer currents. She is the teacher who tricks others into learning.
7		ISHANA-MA Goddess of beauty, grace and elegance. She facilitates the peaceful interaction among her children for harmonious co-habitation. She is a mediator and promotes joyful cooperation. She is the goddess of self-love.
8		APARA-TuRA Goddess of cycles. She is the operator who opens doors for cycles that areopening and closes doors for cycles that are closing. She celebrates the beginning and end of cycles.
9		HAY-LEEM-A Goddess of resources. She is the weigher of the consequences of today's actions on all life, including nature and future generations.
10		UR-U-AMA Goddess of creativity and inspiration. She knows true art inspires altered perception and that life should be lived creatively.
11		AMARAKU Goddess of new beginnings and forging new ways. When the old is gone, she invents a new approach. She is the innovator.
12		ALU-MI-NA Goddess who guards the unknowable. She guards the source of all spiritual knowledge from being accessed by those with impure motives. She is the gatekeeper who determines who may cross.
13		ARA-KA-NA Goddess of the power to transcend all boundaries. She is the guardian of the portal or passageway between Creator and Creation. She represents the gateway hidden within the core of human DNA that enables us to become the I AM that I AM.

Discourse 16
The Fate of Humanity

Q. Why is there such a core feeling of despair in the hearts of people everywhere?

A. Firstly, they believe the past to be unchangeable and the cause of the present. The past changes, moment by moment, as we evolve our awareness in the present. It could therefore be said that the present is the cause of the past. If we do not understand this, we become victimized by the past, carrying its pain with us.

Q. What other causes are there for the despair?

A. There are multiple crossroads in each person's life. These junctions are crucial points on our timeline, where we need to change directions, to reinvent our lives. Most people don't take the cues that it's time to change our lives, but fall back in their old patterns, creating cycles that repeat over and over…

Q. Why would they not take the opportunity to change, rather than repeat the old?

A. When our journey comes to a crossroad, a lot of the past falls away. The fear comes from not knowing which way to go on and what lies ahead, or what is our next step. The despair comes from not being brave enough to take the next step, therefore stepping backwards and trapping ourselves in a repetitive cycle.

Q. Can you give us an example of that?

A. Rebirth cycles: repeating life and death, over and over. When we do a cycle many times, we come to believe that it's inevitable. Death is not inevitable; it's a result of not deciding to change directions at the crossroads. Resurrection is the direction change and the way out of the fishbowl.

Q. What do you think is the biggest reason for despair?

A. Mankind is destroying his own habitat: the Earth. In his heart, man knows he is an endangered species. The Earth will always recover, but in two generations' time, the quality of the land, water, and air will not be sustaining a quality environment for humans. Much of the deterioration that has been set in motion is already non-reversible. The more enlightened the person, the deeper the despair at the folly of man to push his own species to the brink of extinction. This crossroads is the biggest one man has faced.

Q. Would you say the material you've brought forth is responsive to this dilemma?

A. The scientists agree that some of these ecological threats are at this point irreversible, such as the melting of the ice caps. But the salvation of man does not lie in the hands of scientists; it rests on the shoulders of the god beings in the flesh – the light bearers of the planet.

The journey I have walked with the lightfamily who have responded to this work, has been to prepare them for this task.

Q. How can they do this?

A. One can't outrun an avalanche or a sandstorm. The only way to not get caught in it is to go upwards, like being airlifted out of its way.

Q. You mean like transcending to another reality?

A. Exactly. We have to shift a few to a higher reality, and like the 100th monkey syndrome, they pull the rest with them into a more evolved reality.

Q. How many have to be able to elevate their lives to this higher reality for them to be able to lift mankind into a different future?

A. It doesn't take that many. When a higher being, like a god being, comes into a reality of lesser evolutionary levels, they can have a powerful archetypal effect. They can have the beneficial influence of about a thousand humans for instance, if not more. This is the reason that beings from the god kingdom came to save humanity.

Q. But why don't they remember who they are? Why walk in forgetfulness among man?

A. Firstly, if they remember they're not human, they would withdraw, and intermingling with humanity is essential for their mission.

Q. Are there any other reasons?

A. Seeing the species of the Earth with fresh, new eyes, these high ones can appreciate their beauty. Appreciation is a gift that allows the object of ones appreciation to thrive: a principle that the Native Americans practiced in leaving a tobacco offering in exchange for gifts they receive, like when they pick sage or sweet grass.

But this reality's environment seems to lack luster with comparison to the way it looks in a higher reality. If they remember that, there isn't appreciation, but pain over what seems to be lost.

Q. If I look at a tree, what way would it seem different in a higher level of existence?

A. It would seem more vibrant and glowing from within.

Q. Any other reasons why these high ones would be in a position of thinking they're human?

A. They are able to repair the human grid by being part of its program. Man was once a far more conscious and magical being, called Pristine Human. It's ironic that those who are not human, but think they are, are here to help teach humans how to be an evolved human through example.

Q. How does an example teach humans? Or should they go out and teach?

A. Since they're part of the human program, they can change that program by living pristine lives that are free from ego-identification and social conditioning.

Q. What exactly is a grid?

A. It's like a computer software program. It consists of an array of invisible lines of light that overlap a species like a spider web, telling it how to be and how to live. The birds have a grid, for instance, that tells them how to be a bird.

Q. Why is man's grid damaged?

A. Multiple reasons such as global catastrophes that have happened over the ages, aliens inbreeding and interference with man, and abortions after the first three months of pregnancy.

Q. What about toxins like botox?

A. They weaken the grid, but they don't punch holes in it like the self-genocide of abortion.

Q. What would be the way to live this higher reality, and to become saviors for humanity?

A. By creating heaven on Earth everywhere you go. With this as the primary goal of existence, ask yourself, "How would I live if I was in heaven"? The result would be living reverently, as though you're in a sacred site.

Q. Give an example please.

A. You would honor the validity of all species that you encounter there. You would step reverently, knowing the very ground that you walk on is holy ground. When others want to argue with you, the predominant thought would be that one doesn't argue in a holy cathedral, and from that larger perspective, many things people argue about just don't matter. By feeling in touch with the timelessness of existence, even impatience melts away.

If you can live a life like that, free from agendas, and fully aware and present in the moment, you are fulfilling such a holy and lofty destiny: becoming a savior of man.

Discourse 17
The Ceremony of Planetary Transcendence

THE SIGIL OF THE NEWLY EVOKED ANGEL
GOD OF GRACEFUL UNFOLDMENT THROUGH
MIRACULOUS TRANSCENDENCE

Our lightfamily asked how they could support the Planetary Transcendence. Almine received a ceremony in answer to the question, and asked that it be performed at retreats in locations around the world.

The purpose of this ceremony is to repair and heal the etheric tears created during previous cycles of history, specifically the Roman Empire and the so-called Holy Wars, leading into the Dark Ages.

- Due to the tears, entities from the underworlds have been able to gain access to the Earth.

- This ceremony purifies, dissolves and releases the entities while simultaneously creating an opening for Planetary Transcendence.

- It heals the emotional body of the planet into a resurrected field.

As we sit in a circle, our ceremony will create a standing wave form to help our planet and humanity to ascend into a resurrected field.

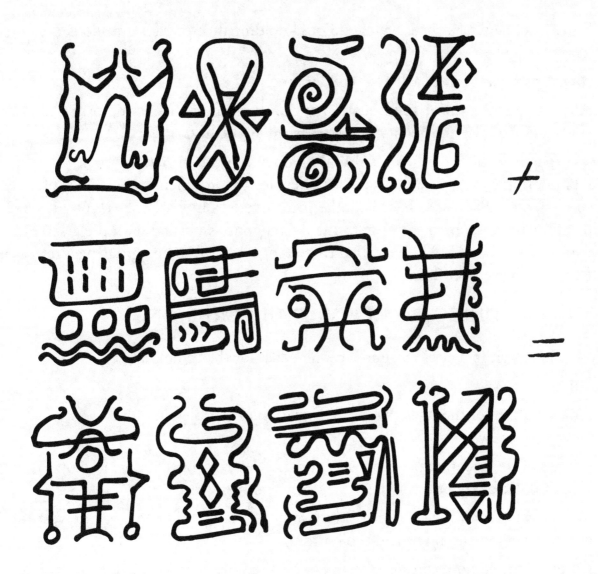

TOOLS FOR THE CEREMONY

- **Sigil:** The Newly Evoked Angel god of Unfoldment through Miraculous Transcendence

  Angel god name: Trihunach-Usetvi-Manurech

- **Alchemical Equation:** The Equation of the Blessing of a New Tomorrow (Purpose: To raise this reality into a transcended reality)

- **441 Angel gods** (See pages 146-149 for names as given in *Book of Spells*, representing DNA Rose A petals/chambers for the experiential capacities of outer space. Note: DNA Rose B which etherically overlays DNA Rose A, contains 672 petals/chambers which correlate to the Angel gods associated with the 7 sets of Runes. 7 x 96 = 672. Almine called these Angel gods into being during a retreat in Russia in November 2014.)

DIRECTIONS FOR THE CEREMONY

Have participants sit in a circle around a center stack for the ceremony.

Center stack:

1. At the bottom of the stack place The Equation of the Blessing for a New Tomorrow.

2. On top of the equation place the sigil for the Newly Evoked Angel god of Graceful Unfoldment through Miraculous Transcendence.

3. On the very top of the stack place the list of 441 names of angel gods (lowest numbers on top and highest at the bottom).

4. Listen to the audio recording of Almine for the introduction to and performance of the ceremony: available as an MP3 download (see the front of this book to access download).

Discourse 18
Fluid Manifestation of Divine Intent

Q. As humanity transcends, they seem to enter a spiritual maturity, if I understand you correctly. They are able to manifest a reality based on inspiration: the voice of Infinite Intent...

A. Yes, that's right.

Q. Well, is the human body 'wired' for these advanced functions? Do they slumber within, the way the capacities of an adult slumber in a baby?

A. The physical body has the 'wiring,' or components, waiting to shift into evolved and higher functioning. Today the baby may just be able to grab his rattle, but one day he will be able to catch a football.

Q. Name some components that will be able to assist with manifesting our chosen realities.

A. The "12 Ordinary Meridians from the Womb of Fluid Manifestation of Infinite Intent," which is why so much emphases and so many tools have been devoted to prepare the 12 Main, or Ordinary Meridians, for their higher function (see www.fragrancealchemy.com for the alchemical oils and protocol for the purification of the twelve meridians).

Q. What prompts their awakening to a higher function?

A. The seed lies dormant in the ground until the Song of Spring tells it that it's time to wake up. In a resurrected reality there are new, advanced frequencies, not encountered in lower realities as being something that are automatically produced by the Earth and its creatures.

Q. What do you mean by "automatically produced"?

A. Part of raising one reality to the next is to generate the higher reality's frequencies in the lower. But such frequencies of a higher reality are not naturally occurring as part of the lower reality's song.

Q. What frequencies awaken the higher function of the 12 Ordinary Meridians?

A. The twelve Tones of Fluid Manifestation. The eight Extraordinary Meridians set the stage for the manifestation, and the twelve Ordinary Meridians create the play within the parameters of the stage.

Q. What type of stages can be set by the Extraordinary Meridians?

A. For a resurrected being, three stages are set to manifest events within. These stages come in the spotlight during certain times of the day.

1. Noon – 8 pm: the stage of Spiritual Mastery, godhood.
2. 8 pm – 4 am: the stage of Pristine Humanity, the purification of human affairs.
3. 4 am – noon: the stage of the Miraculous, of living beyond boundaries, super godhood.

Q. If I need a miracle, I would therefore focus on its manifestation preferably between 4 am and noon?

A. Yes. It's available at all times but more emphasized then, in the same way that during spiritual evolution, we don't actually leave a stage behind to graduate to the next. The previous stage is still there but the spotlight (our awareness) is just emphasizing a different way of living in a higher reality, with different possibilities.

Q. Is there a deeper reason behind this division of manifesting in different realities?

A. Yes, angels provide a good example: the mightiest angels are able to profoundly affect life in the etheric but are very rarely able to manifest even a loaf of bread in the physical. Beings from the Hidden Realms want to help, but to affect physical life directly is seldom possible.

Q. Can angels help our lives at all?

A. They set events in motion by beneficially affecting the etheric realms. But there's a delay, and sometimes we inadvertently work against such manifestation through our fear and doubts.

Q. How else do we block beneficial manifestation?

A. By addiction to tension. Many are afraid of the expansion they feel when they enter surrendered trust, so they welcome adversity and tension.

Q. What are the twelve Tones of Fluid Manifestation?

A. They are:

1. Inspiration
2. Receptiveness
3. Self-determination
4. Omni-perspectives
5. Self-support
6. Self-assurance
7. Harmony
8. Creativity
9. Flexibility
10. Fertility
11. Humor
12. Rapture

Added together, they form an alchemical equation that adds up to Fluid Manifestation, the Tone of the Resurrected, Transcended life.

Q. What else prevents the fluid energy from flowing along the 12 meridians?

A. Guilt, age-old themes of feelings of guilt and failure. To shed guilt is one of the primary challenges that must be met for transcending into a resurrected life.

Q. By age-old, do you mean the themes of guilt have followed us through the ages?

A. Yes. In an area of Siberia around a lake, one person a week goes missing. They are hunted and devoured by a prehistoric creature that lives in the lake, capsizing boats and following its prey even onto the shore. Sonar shows it to be approximately 16 meters, or 48 feet, in length. A prehistoric remnant of the dinosaur age, it can breathe under water through slits in its neck, and hide in underground tunnels that link the lake with other lakes.

There are in fact, eight of these prehistoric monsters that for some reason have plagued us through the ages. Through perception, they can be dissolved, releasing the necessary energy for transcendence to occur.

Q. Please share them. What are these eight areas of guilt?

A. The areas of guilt are:

1. The guilt of having injured others through 'wrong' choices. But don't forget that we have previously been guided by adversity. When we provided others with adversity, it can also be said that we provided them with guidance. Life moves through us in mysterious ways, there are no mistakes. All of life is innocent.

2. Guilt of causing the demise of other beings. As our light gets brighter through the overcoming of illusion in our lives, beings of shadow disappear. We created them by the occlusions, or blind spots, in our vision. We uncreate them by overcoming those illusions.

3. The guilt of the loss of power to help heal our environment. The deep guilt of feeling diminished and helpless comes from remembering the time when we were able to exert influence on our environment to a much larger extent. But we have transfigured from formlessness, to etheric form, to physical form. The contraction into matter binds up power to maintain the density of matter – a necessary part of our journey.

4. Guilt over the decaying process of aging, when we know at the depth of our being that we are timeless and eternal. Aging is the destructuring of the obsolete, to make way for the unfolding of the new. It was never meant as a permanent state of being but rather a transient, transitionary one. Only because of programming, and the fact that what we resist persists, does aging remain.

5. Guilt over our dependency on external provisions and materialistic items like medicines, calculators, clothing, transportation and much more. In material form, our visionary abilities are greatly decreased. Material items compensate for this. Unlike the Australian aboriginal, who can tell details of astronomy from visionary experiences, we use a telescope. He can transport his dream body to distant places, while we use an airplane. It is simply the law of compensation at work in the denser levels of life.

6. We feel guilty when we fail to seem lovable to others, or when others reject us. We think the fault lies with us. But the truth is there are only a very few masters who have silenced the inner dialog of the mind. It is impossible to have pure love from an opened heart when the dialog is present. What humanity calls love is a mixture of addiction stemming from the unwholeness within, neediness and duty. Very few can feel true love.

7. Guilt over not being able to support ourselves and survive in our world. Animal species can live off of what their environment supplies but we can't. They are confined to a specific area or eco-system where the conditions support their needs. We have the freedom to be mobile. Ancient man lived off the land but spent most of their short lives engaged in survival. Our lives allow free time that permits opportunities for higher thoughts like philosophy, and quests of the spirit.

8. We feel guilt over inequality: we're safe and fed, and others are not. We are intelligent and fit while others are impaired. It is a judgment to think that others are less fortunate, just because their gifts aren't obvious. The law of compensation in the lower levels of duality is an equalizer, and for every loss there has been a gain, whether it is obvious to us or not. We strengthen that which we focus on and by seeing others' lack rather than their gifts, would strengthen that aspect.

In the symphony of life, if all notes played at once there would be no music. The melody is created as much by the notes that play, as the ones that don't. Honor the ones who seem to lack, for their unique contribution to the Song of Existence. Somewhere along the unfolding, never-ending symphony of life, their note will one day yet again play.

Discourse 19
Guidance for a New Reality

Q. What affirmation do you recommend for a life that has transcended beyond the opposition of duality?

A. "May I be released from the binding ties of previous dreams. May I manifest a life of deep peace and support, and from within it, my passion and inspiration." I have stated it as a prayer, but it becomes an affirmation when you form it into a positive statement.

Q. You have mentioned that personal labels and a sense of identity obstruct personal growth and retard evolution of consciousness. What about the personality? Is it part of the identities that we cultivate?

A. Most beings in this density are in identity consciousness. It is useful when, as humans, we study the unique aspects of our being – the specific idiosyncrasies of our individuation.

As we graduate into oneness, the preparatory stage for godhood, we must lose egoic identification. Personality can still remain because it's different than personal labels of identification. Personality can be considered the dust of the ages. It consists of the coping mechanisms of learned behavior that we cultivate over the ages as we interact with our environment. These must be shed as we transcend into a resurrected life.

Q. Is there a specific reason that this stage requires its release?

A. The stage of transcending into resurrected life requires that it be a life guided by inspiration, which is the voice of Divine, or Infinite, intent. If old coping programs are motiving our conduct, it obscures these whispers from within, as well as our authentic responses to them.

Q. What does this stage prepare us for?

A. An advanced stage of godhood that I described in the book *Secrets of the Hidden Realms***. I call it super godhood.

** See *Secrets of the Hidden Realms,* www.spiritualjourneys.com.

Q. How has the Earth's and humanity's rapid evolution affected other star systems?

A. As the Earth evolved, many races evolved also because of the Earth's very important archetypal role. Some races lived at levels of consciousness too low to make the shift and were pulled into oblivion. The key date was August 2005, when the Earth broke free from old cycles of illusion.

Q. Did they foresee it coming?

A. Races could see that after August 2005, their race had no future to time travel to. They could see that the epicenter and pivot point of this cosmic purging was the Earth and its progress.

Q. Is that why the abductions took place, to try and interbreed with man to ensure that a part of them would survive?

A. Yes, but also to prevent benevolent races from assisting us by suppressing information about UFO encounters.

Q. Give an example please.

A. In the 1970's a group of pale-skinned, very tall men, dressed in black would threaten people if they disclosed their UFO encounters.

Q. Who were the men in black?

A. They were humanoid-looking creatures that were especially, genetically engineered by the grey creatures from the planet in the belt of Orion, Zeta Reticuli, for this purpose.

Q. Are they still here?

A. They disappeared after August 2005 along with many races from Orion. They left behind holograms of themselves that appear where they are studied, even though their physical presence is no longer here.

Q. How can these holograms be cleansed from the Earth?

A. It is like a past nightmare that still lingers. As we as individuals, allow our past to be seen as a dream, and release its influence on us in the present, so will this nightmare on Earth also melt away.

THE SEVEN BODIES OF MAN

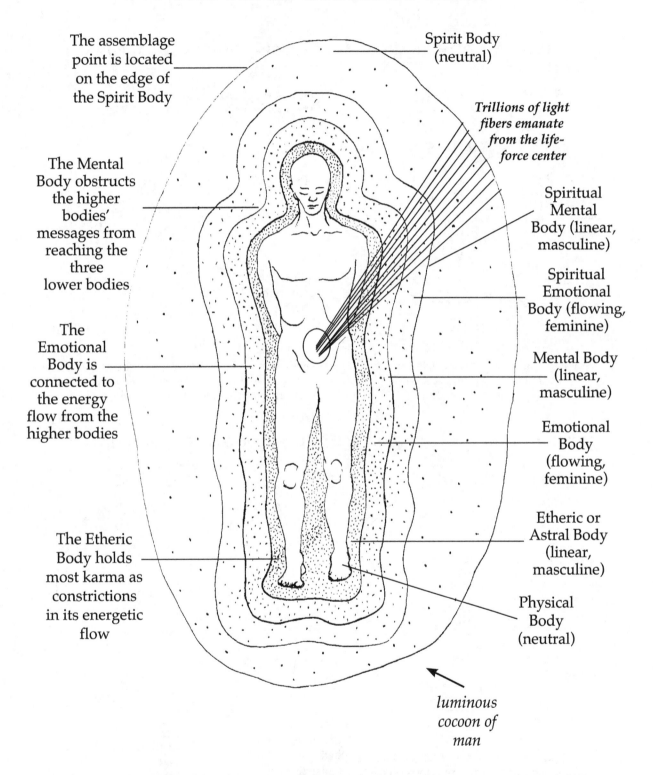

The assemblage point is located on the edge of the Spirit Body

The Mental Body obstructs the higher bodies' messages from reaching the three lower bodies

The Emotional Body is connected to the energy flow from the higher bodies

The Etheric Body holds most karma as constrictions in its energetic flow

Spirit Body (neutral)

Trillions of light fibers emanate from the life-force center

Spiritual Mental Body (linear, masculine)

Spiritual Emotional Body (flowing, feminine)

Mental Body (linear, masculine)

Emotional Body (flowing, feminine)

Etheric or Astral Body (linear, masculine)

Physical Body (neutral)

luminous cocoon of man

The bodies are superimposed over each other and form the luminous cocoon of man. The trillions of light fibers from the life force center penetrate all other bodies.

PHASES WITHIN THE GOD KINGDOMS

GOD-KINGDOM PHASE 2

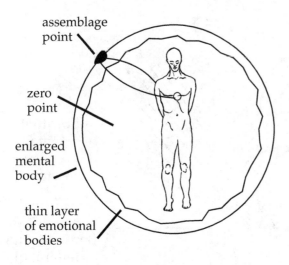

assemblage point

zero point

enlarged mental body

thin layer of emotional bodies

Very few emotions are felt during this phase. Mental body rotates the same as in phase 1.

SUPER-GOD-KINGDOM PHASE 1

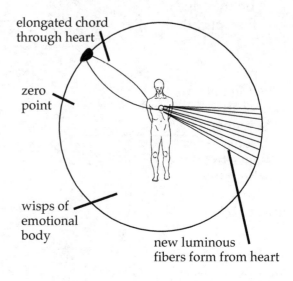

elongated chord through heart

zero point

wisps of emotional body

new luminous fibers form from heart

Fields are 6 times the length of the physical body. Mental body has partial rotations alternating clockwise/counter clockwise.

SUPER-GOD-KINGDOM PHASE 2

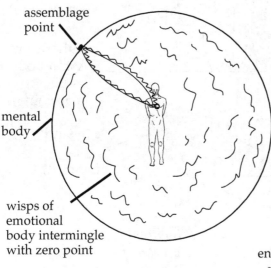

assemblage point

mental body

wisps of emotional body intermingle with zero point

Fields are now 50 times larger. The luminous fibers from previous phase have now thickened the cord.

SUPER-GOD-KINGDOM PHASE 3

enlarged zero point with smoke-like substance within consisting of mental, emotional, and awareness components of next stage

Fields are 360 times larger. Chord is stretched thin again and solid mental body is gone.

Q. How can we release the hold of our pasts?

A. Our past shapes our identities and belief systems. Let those go and much of the past goes with it. There are two affirmations that I can recommend to repeat daily:

1. I am a being as vast as the cosmos, having a human experience.
2. I believe in nothing. Through effortless knowing, I access all I need to know in the moment.

Q. Tell us about how it feels, or what to expect, in the 3 stages of resurrection?

A. Firstly, during the three stages of identity consciousness, the two stages of oneness, and the first two of the three stages of resurrection, a point directly at the top of the nose, between the brows is used. This center is called the Isabach, and it helps us determine spatial ups and downs. It's like the body's gyroscope. After the third stage of resurrection there is a period of vertigo, and an inability to focus the eyes well, while the brain forms new connections and pathways to relate to space differently.

Q. Is there something we can do in advance to ease this transition and start the formation of the new pathways?

A. Yes, *Shrihat Satva, The Yoga to Clear Past Incarnations* (see www.spiritualjourneys.com book section).

Q. Are the extrasensory senses heightened during this third stage of resurrection? There are cases of people surviving a lightning strike and finding that from the new brain connections that form as the brain tries to heal itself, that they've become extraordinarily psychic.

A. Yes, there isn't much difference in the first two stages of resurrection, possibly because those aren't the stages in which the new brain connections form. However there is a difference in the third stage, particularly with the sense of clairvoyance. It seems to greatly increase.

Q. But extreme clairvoyance is said to become a nuisance in that all the ghosts in the environment become visible, and once they know that the clairvoyant can see them, they flock to that person.

A. It isn't that highly developed, just enough to be life enhancing, or it would be uncomfortable. There are far more ghosts than people realize everywhere.

As we release past accomplishments and failure as that which gives us identity, they too will be released.

Q. You have said that the first stage's challenge is always fear, as we move from rung to rung up the evolutionary ladder. Is there anything we can do to ease that during the first stage of resurrection?

A. The fear during the initial stages of major evolutionary shifts is just something we have to ride through. It helps to know why it's there, that it's indicative of a step forward. Breathe deeply through the panic attacks – Arasatma breathing[††] techniques help.

Q. You have said that the first stage of resurrection is the combining of life and death, of the body and the soul. What do the other stages do?

A. Firstly, the three stages jointly unite the body with its components (that which people generally refer to as the higher self and the highest self). This creates an incorruptible body made of spiritualized matter.

The first stage combines the body and soul. The second and third stages combine the two levels of spirit, and spiritualized matter forms.

Q. Why have these pieces separated in the first place?

A. Because pieces were lost and forgotten, and we descended into gross matter like sediment falling to the bottom. These pieces need to be retrieved for us to be whole enough to unite and integrate all of our components.

During the first stage of resurrection, we unite with our soul, or dream body. During the second and the third stage, we unite with the two layers of our spirit. This is done by clearing out the unconscious, right brain mind. Then cleaning out the subconscious, heart mind.

Q. What do you mean, 'clearing out'?

A. We have to face our fears, pain, and guilt by resolving it through perception. These areas of negative emotions have shaped our individual perspectives and determined our life's choices. As they spill into our everyday life, our emotions become heightened in order for us to detect areas of constriction, and to resolve their illusions.

Q. We have to physically experience a death equivalent for the first resurrection to occur, and life and death to unite. If we visit the soul world, or place of death, during the first stage – what about the other two stages?

A. There's no need to visit other realms for these two…

---

†† See *The Sacred Breaths of Arasatma*, www.spiritualjourneys.com.

Q. But you had to. You descended into the underworld, and then the lower underworld?

A. The planetary resurrection requires the same steps. But if the planet herself descended into these realms to resolve the negativity held there, it would have spilled into humanity, and the terror and pain would have dragged everyone's consciousness back down. I can assure you, it was almost unbearable.

Q. What is the meaning of life?

A. Does it have to have a meaning? Life is for our deep enjoyment, through focused awareness of its many miracles.

Discourse 20
The Restoration of the Magic Life

Q. Why are so many people on antidepressants? Even among college students, the statistics are quite concerning.

A. There is a topic that is mostly ignored by professionals and teachers alike: The drudgery and tedium of daily life. When people inevitably encounter it, they are diagnosed as depressed and given medication to deal with it. But it doesn't go away and so it returns to rear its head again.

Q. Why does the drudgery exist? And also, what is drudgery?

A. Drudgery can be defined as an attempt to combat inertia. I have found two types of inertia – a proactive and a passive inertia. In separation consciousness, inertia is proactive: It requires that it be fed energy on a continual basis, just to maintain the status quo, just to retain what we've achieved.

It's like rolling a rock up hill. One has to keep it from rolling backwards by exerting constant pressure. There is a saying: Life is a journey, not a camp. One is either going forwards or backwards depending on how well your passion can overcome the inertia.

Q. Where does the passive inertia fit in?

A. When one enters the stage of losing egocentricity, becoming one with all things, the passive inertia results from the deep bliss that lures one into inactivity and lack of motivation. If one succumbs, their personal power and consciousness drain away.

Q. For the masses, the drudgery comes therefore from realizing that they have to keep pushing the rock of life, or it will roll down the mountain? It's the ultimate example of work that never gets done. That truly is depressing, since one has nothing to show for it at the end of one's life.

A. A battle well fought is its own reward. The reason for this is the inner strength it gives. Physical life in duality is like the bean sprout, fighting its way upward into the sun. It cannot see what lies beyond as it battles its way upward through the opposing soil, it only knows that not to do so, is to perish. But this preparatory stage gives it the strength to withstand the wind and the rain as it emerges as a bean plant.

Q. If drudgery is the response we feel when we encounter inertia as a cosmic principle present in duality-based realities, how can we handle the depression?

A. I have noticed that those who thrive are those who take personal responsibility for their own well-being. Only you can change your life from tragic to magic.

Q. How?

A. Firstly, personal tragedies or illness can interrupt the production of serotonin and other feel good hormones. This is particularly the case for women who have just given birth – the placenta provides these hormones during pregnancy – and once it's expelled as afterbirth and before she can produce her own, is usually a very depressing time.

Q. What do you recommend to help stimulate and encourage our own serotonin production?

A. A cup of St. John's Wort tea, once a day for two months is helpful, as are homeopathic remedies that are designed to stimulate our feel good hormone production. The point that I wish to emphasize is that although I'd like to discuss long-term methods of having a joyous and magical life, intervention is necessary in acute cases where our own bodily systems for maintaining our well being are derailed.

Q. In the perfection of existence, you have often said, "the purpose of life is enjoyment". Surely life has provided a means by which this can be a journey of joy?

A. It did provide a way and it can be ours if we claim it. It brings online three areas of the brain, which through misuse, lie dormant. These three areas are: the Broca region, the Wernicke area and the planum temporalis. We can have magical manifestations and revelations to bring the joy of the magical life into our journey. The restoration of magic replaces the drudgery. The quality of the journey is so enhanced that it doesn't matter that it has no end, or is repetitive.

Q. What do these newly activated brain regions do?

A. The Wernicke region promotes harmlessness through heightened sympathetic empathy...

Q. What does that mean?

A. We become so sensitive to the feelings of all life forms so that to hurt another is to hurt ourselves.

Q. What about the Broca region? And the planum temporalis?

A. The Broca region awakens the frequencies of nature within us. The planum temporalis dissolves logical expectations through the magical perspective. These three areas are integrally connected. Becoming empathically attuned to nature requires harmlessness, and one becomes more harmless, the more empathically sensitive they become...

Q. ...and the planum temporalis?

A. In order to see the magical world, one must first see the natural world.

Q. You have previously mentioned that the high heart is the gateway to the magical life?

A. What stands between us and the magical awakening of our world are the illusions that we have concerning space and time. The high heart senses the fluid nature of matter and space. It intuits that the moment is but a snapshot of intent moving through eternity.

Q. You once said that the corpus callosum, the piece in the brain that bridges left and right hemispheres, has an unexplained significance in our spiritual evolution. What is this role?

A. It is a role that coordinates with the three newly awakened areas in the brain as we cultivate the magical perspective. The magic life approaches its world by combining inner and outer space. The activation of the corpus callosum's higher function allows us to see deeply behind the appearances without, and feel deeply the true nature of what we're experiencing within. Let's say that it gives us depth perception.

Q. How so?

A. Let's define what a reality is: It's a mapped out section of the field of potential that we wish to examine through experience. It takes three points to map out a two-dimensional triangle of reality to explore. But if you want a more three-dimensional experience of a reality, you need a fourth point to form a pyramid.

The corpus callosum is that fourth point that creates depth to our inner and outer experiences. Like the tip of a pyramid, it can go as deep into our experiences as we want. The deeper we probe the mysteries of our existence, the wider the application of our magic.

Q. This journey we have been on then has been an in-depth study into the mysteries of life. Are you saying that it empowers us to broadly affect our environment?

A. Yes, that's right.

Q. The magical perspectives: does that mean we are looking for magical occurrences?

A. To look for miraculous manifestations blocks entry into the magical life. Be aware of them with gratitude, but seek instead to sense the magical essence within all life. This inner exploration of life is done through our inner senses' response. Life responds magically to such an approach.

Q. What message can you give lightworkers to help life them up and over the drudgery of everyday life?

A. There is no drudgery anywhere. Life is a miraculous journey of ever-new discoveries. Drudgery is an illusion conjured up by the unaware and those who have lost their vision, and the poetry in their hearts.

It is true that we are encountering a destructuring of many societal values that we have held dear. This is always the case before a huge evolutionary shift, or at the end of an age-old cycle. It could be easy to succumb to the despair of the world. But in the burnt out, blackened field of civilizations crumbling, a single blade of new, green grass pushes through the ashes. Before our appreciative awareness, it flourishes into spring. Choose to see the magic of new beginnings. You are the bringers of a new tomorrow, you are the holy ones of the Earth.

CLOSING

Within every question slumbers an answer. Yet man has avoided asking many deep questions about his role in the universe, and the burdens of humanity, upon this journey. Their avoidance stems from the fear that these questions may be unanswerable, and that this may deepen the despair in the hearts of humankind at feeling alone and adrift in the vastness of space.

Man's role as a powerful catalyst of change for all life, is a significant one. It has been obscured from man for eons of time, denying him the comfort of knowing that each individual life matters profoundly, contributing its unique gifts to complete the perfection of unfolding life. The answers in this book have parted the veil that has hidden the great and noble role of man. They have provided a message of hope and a clearer understanding that the one can beneficially affect the many: changing life from tragic, to magic.

CPSIA information can be obtained
at www.ICGtesting.com
Printed in the USA
BVHW062116030619

550068BV00002B/3/P